Cambridge Certificate in Advanced English 3
with answers

Cambridge Certificate in Advanced English 3

WITH ANSWERS

Examination papers from the University of Cambridge Local Examinations Syndicate

CAMBRIDGE
UNIVERSITY PRESS

CAMBRIDGE UNIVERSITY PRESS
Cambridge, New York, Melbourne, Madrid, Cape Town, Singapore, São Paulo

Cambridge University Press
The Edinburgh Building, Cambridge CB2 2RU, UK

www.cambridge.org
Information on this title: www.cambridge.org/9780521797672

First published 1995
Second edition 2001
5th printing 2006

Printed in the United Kingdom at the University Press, Cambridge

A catalogue record for this publication is available from the British Library

ISBN-13 978-0-521-79767-2 Student's Book with answers
ISBN-10 0-521-79767-5 Student's Book with answers

ISBN-13 978-0-521-79766-5 Student's Book
ISBN-10 0-521-79766-7 Student's Book

ISBN-13 978-0-521-79768-9 Teacher's Book
ISBN-10 0-521-79768-3 Teacher's Book

ISBN-13 978-0-521-79769-6 Set of 2 Cassettes
ISBN-10 0-521-79769-1 Set of 2 Cassettes

Contents

Acknowledgements

The publishers are grateful to the following for permission to reproduce copyright material. It has not always been possible to identify the sources of all the material used and in such cases the publishers would welcome information from the copyright owners.

The *Independent* for the articles by Danny Danziger on p. 8 and Liz Hodgkinson on p. 27; Explore Worldwide for the text on pp. 11–12; Octopus for the extract from *Encyclopaedia of Natural History* by Joyce Pope; extracts on p. 24 and pp. 62–63 from *Which?*, published by Consumers' Association, 2 Marylebone Road, London NW1 4DF; for further information phone 0800 252 100; *The Guardian* for the articles on pp. 32–33 by Edward Greenfield, pp. 34–35 by Winston Fletcher and pp. 37–38 from *New Internationalist* © *The Guardian*; PFD for the text on p. 45 adapted from an extract from *Awful Moments* by Philip Norman (© Philip Norman 1986), reprinted by permission of PFD on behalf of Philip Norman; Premiere Media Press for the text on p. 57 by Christopher Matthew from British Airways *Highlife Magazine* (March 1992); The National Magazine Company for the text on pp. 58–59 adapted from *Country Living* April 1992 © National Magazine Company; A. M. Heath and Holt Associates Inc. for the text on p. 76 from *How Children Fail* by John Holt (Copyright © John Holt) by permission of A. M. Heath & Co Ltd and Holt Associates Inc. © 2000; *The Observer* for the text on p. 83 © *The Observer*; *The BBC Wildlife Magazine* for the text on p. 86 by Angela Turner; *The Telegraph* for the text on pp. 88–89 © Telegraph Group Ltd; Breslich & Foss for the text on p. 96 from *Herbs and Spices* by Gail Duff; Egmont Children's Books for the text on p. 102 from *Let's go Fishing*.

For permission to reproduce photographs: pp. C1 and C2: all pictures from Robert Harding Picture Library, photographers as follows: 1.5C and 1.5Q M. H. Black; 1.5D and 1.5R, 1.5F and 1.5L, 1.5G and 1.5N, 1.5H and 1.5M, 1.5I and 1.5O Roy Rainford; 1.5E and 1.5P Raj Kamal; 1.5J and 1.5K Philip Craven; p. C3 (top) Lincolnshire County Council: Usher Gallery, Lincoln, (bottom) Recreation, Leisure and Tourism Department, City of Lincoln; p. C4 (top left) Newcastle Evening Chronicle, (top right) Science Photolibrary, (bottom left and centre left) Alex Bartel/Science Photolibrary, (bottom right) Telegraph Colour Library; p. C5 (top left) Telegraph Colour Library, (top right) Liba Taylor/Panos Pictures, (bottom left) Trygne Bølstad/Panos Pictures, (centre right) Popperfoto Ltd, (bottom right) A. Warren/Telegraph Colour Library; p. C8 (top left) Popperfoto Ltd, (top right) Robert Harding Picture Library, (centre left) Paul von Stoheim/Telegraph Colour Library; p. C9 Chris Stowers/Panos Pictures, (centre left) by permission of Barclay's Bank plc, (centre right) Jacqui and Peter Sanger/ Telegraph Colour Library, (bottom right) Telegraph Colour Library; p. C10 (bottom right) Telegraph Colour Library, all remaining pictures on this page: Robert Harding Picture Library, photographer (bottom left) Walter Rawlings, (top right) Gavin Hellier; pp. C14 and C15 London Borough of Barnet; p. C16 (left) Popperfoto Ltd.

We are unable to trace the copyright owners of photographs on pp. C6, C7, C11, C12, (centre and right) C16, and would be grateful for any information, which will enable us to do so.

Text artwork by Virginia Gray, Peter Ducker and UCLES
Design concept by Peter Ducker [M S T D]

Cover design by Dunne & Scully

The cassettes which accompany this book were recorded at Studio AVP, London.

To *the student*

This book is for candidates preparing for the University of Cambridge Local Examinations Syndicate (UCLES) Certificate in Advanced English (CAE) examination. It contains four complete tests based on past papers which have been adapted to reflect the most recent CAE specifications (introduced in December 1999).

The CAE examination is part of a group of examinations developed by UCLES called the Cambridge Main Suite. The Main Suite consists of five examinations which have similar characteristics but which are designed for different levels of English language ability. Within the five levels, CAE is at Cambridge Level 4.

Cambridge Level 5 Certificate of Proficiency in English (CPE)
Cambridge Level 4 Certificate in Advanced English (CAE)
Cambridge Level 3 First Certificate in English (FCE)
Cambridge Level 2 Preliminary English Test (PET)
Cambridge Level 1 Key English Test (KET)

The CAE examination consists of five papers:

Paper 1	Reading	1 hour 15 minutes
Paper 2	Writing	2 hours
Paper 3	English in Use	1 hour 30 minutes
Paper 4	Listening	45 minutes (approximately)
Paper 5	Speaking	15 minutes

Paper 1   Reading
This paper consists of four parts, each containing one text or several shorter pieces. The texts are taken from newspapers, magazines, non-literary books, leaflets, brochures, etc., and are selected to test a wide range of reading skills and strategies. There are between 40 and 50 multiple matching, multiple choice and gapped text questions in total.

Paper 2 Writing

This paper consists of two writing tasks (e.g. letter, report, review, instructions, announcement, etc.) of approximately 250 words each. **Part 1** consists of one compulsory task based on a substantial reading input. **Part 2** consists of one task selected from a choice of four. Question 5 is always business related. Assessment is based on content, organisation and cohesion, accuracy and range of language, register and effect on target reader.

Paper 3 English in Use

This paper consists of six tasks designed to test the ability to apply knowledge of the language system, including vocabulary, grammar, spelling and punctuation, word-building, register and cohesion. It contains 80 items in total.

Part 1 is based on a short text and consists of a four-option multiple-choice cloze which focuses on vocabulary.

Part 2 is based on a short text and consists of a gap-fill exercise at word level which focuses on grammar.

Part 3 is based on a short text and is designed to test the ability to proofread and correct samples of written English. There are two types of task, either of which may be used in a test. In the first, candidates have to identify additional words which are incorporated in the text. In the second, candidates have to identify errors of spelling and punctuation.

Part 4 is based on two short texts and consists of a gap-fill exercise which focuses on word-building.

Part 5 is based on two short texts; the first text provides the input for the second text, which is a gap-fill exercise. This task focuses on the ability to re-write a given text in a different register.

Part 6 is based on a short text and consists of a gap-fill exercise at phrase or sentence level.

Paper 4 Listening

This paper consists of four texts of varying length and nature which test a wide range of listening skills. There are between 30 and 40 matching, completion and multiple-choice questions in total.

Paper 5 Speaking

Candidates are examined in pairs by two examiners, one taking the part of the interlocutor and the other of the assessor. The four parts of the test, which are based on visual stimuli and verbal prompts, are designed to elicit a wide range of speaking skills and strategies from both candidates.

Candidates are assessed individually. The assessor focuses on grammar and vocabulary, discourse management, pronunciation, and interactive communication. The interlocutor provides a global mark for the whole test.

Marks and results

The five CAE papers total 200 marks, after weighting. Each paper is weighted to 40 marks.

Your overall CAE grade is based on the total score gained in all five papers. It is not necessary to achieve a satisfactory level in all five papers in order to pass the examination. Certificates are given to candidates who pass the examination with grade A, B or C. A is the highest. The minimum successful performance in order to achieve Grade C corresponds to about 60% of the total marks. You will be informed if you do particularly well in any individual paper. D and E are failing grades. If you fail, you will be informed about the papers in which your performance was particularly weak.

The CAE examination is recognised by the majority of British universities for English language entrance requirements.

Further information

For more information about CAE or any other UCLES examination write to:

EFL Division
UCLES
1 Hills Road
Cambridge
CB1 2EU
UK

Telephone: +44 1223 553311
Fax: +44 1223 460278
e-mail: efl@ucles.org.uk
http://www.cambridge-efl.org.uk

Test 1

PAPER 1   READING (1 hour 15 minutes)

Part 1

Answer questions **1–14** by referring to the book reviews on page **5**.

For questions **1–14**, match each of the statements below with one of the books **(A–E)** reviewed on page **5**. Some of the choices may be required more than once. Indicate your answers **on the separate answer sheet**.

Note: When more than one answer is required, these may be given **in any order**.

Which book or books

focuses on a character whose lifestyle changes completely?	**1**	
deals with the feelings of different age groups?	**2**	
features a main character growing up in a provincial town?	**3**	
shows the influence of another art form?	**4**	
deal with the beginning of a new enterprise?	**5**	**6** ....
reveals a fondness for the past?	**7**	
explores the development of a long-term relationship?	**8**	
depicts contrasting moods?	**9**	
handle complex relationships with humour?	**10**	**11** ....
focuses on two characters' feelings for the same person?	**12**	
has a main character reluctant to exploit physical attributes?	**13**	
is set in academic circles?	**14**	

Pack a paperback – Holiday reading

A 'I actually look rather good in jeans. So I rarely wear them. I don't want to get mixed up with the wrong sort of person.' So runs the logic of Isabel, 'our heroine' in this refreshingly zany novel. An art student of 31, devotee of historical romances, she seeks Mr Right but is concerned lest her knobbly knees ruin her chances. Hope, however, springs eternal – which proves to be her salvation, and that of other people in the story. Employing the staccato drama-laden pace of an early silent film, with chapter headings like 'Our Hero Feels Inspired', the author writes with terrific verve.

B This is a celebration of the birth and subsequent near-death of a local radio station in America. It is the wry view of a national institution – the wireless – seen through the eyes of a weedy, intelligent child, Francis With. Francis works for WLT (With Lettuce and Tomato) Radio, a station set up by Roy and Ray Soderbjerg to advertise their sandwich bar. Soon the station is beaming out a motley collection of singers, preachers, soap-opera heroes and continuity announcers. This small-town American setting provides the author with huge scope for the dry humour and understated prose for which he is justly praised. He skilfully transports the reader from the present back to the gentler days of the 1940s and 1950s, an era of dime stores, oil-cloth, old-fashioned Ford motor cars and, of course, the wireless.

C In the world created by the author, it is quite in order for a second husband to gossip with his wife's first husband. So, when high-flying professor Richard Vaisey falls for a beautiful Russian poetess, he naturally confides in his wife's ex. The poetess writes rotten poetry, which troubles Richard's critical conscience; she's also trying to get his support for her wrongfully imprisoned brother. However, none of these complications is half as interesting as the way the author untangles them. He moves the plot along with a robust sense of the ridiculous and dissects relationships with perceptive care. It all makes for a highly enjoyable, sophisticated and witty read.

D Two sets of best friends – two women, two men – meet in the London of the sixties, and for the next quarter of a century are bound together in life and death. At the outset of this long novel, one of the four, the mysterious American tycoon, James Hudson, is launching a newspaper, which his friend Richard Blake is editing. The launch is crucial, but so is the fact that the woman they both adored (and that one of them married) was killed some years before… Murder, ambition, love and jealousy – it's all here, and the writing's good as well. This is one of those books, in size and range, where you can really get to know the characters and be engrossed in them.

E Written by one of the very best American fiction writers, this amusing and compassionate story tells how Ian Bedloe, by way of atonement for a sin that leaves him plagued with guilt, becomes 'father' to his brother's three orphaned children. What with the detritus of domesticity, he is, at 40, slowly sinking into eccentric bachelorhood. The story covers much emotional ground and highlights, in particular, the touching, tender relationship Ian develops with the youngest child, Daphne. A lovely, warm book with exactly the right balance of pathos and laughter.

Part 2

For questions **15–20**, choose which of the paragraphs **A–G** on page **7** fit into the numbered gaps in the following magazine article. There is one extra paragraph, which does not fit in any of the gaps.

Indicate your answers **on the separate answer sheet**.

WEATHERVANE MAKER

THE MAKING of weathervanes is an ancient skill, going back to early Egyptian times. Today the craft is still very much alive in the workshop that Graham Smith has set up. He is one of the few people in the country who make hand-cut weathervanes. Graham's designs are individually created and tailored to the specific requirements of his customers. 'That way I can produce a unique personalised item,' he explains. 'A lot of my customers are women buying presents for their husbands. They want a distinctive gift that represents the man's business or leisure interests.'

15

It was not a cockerel but a witch on a broomstick that featured on the first weathervane Graham ever made. Friends admired his surprise present for his wife and began asking him to make vanes for them. 'I realised that when it came to subjects that could be made into them, the possibilities were limitless,' he says.

16

That was five years ago and he has no regrets about his new direction. 'My previous work didn't have an artistic element to it, whereas this is exciting and creative,' he says. 'I really enjoy the design side.'

17

Graham also keeps plenty of traditional designs in stock, since they prove as popular as the one-offs. 'It seems that people are attracted to hand-crafting,' Graham says. 'They welcome the opportunity to acquire something a little bit different.'

18

'I have found my place in the market. People love the individuality and I get a lot of satisfaction from seeing a nondescript shape turn into something almost lifelike,' he says.

19

'And nowadays, with more and more people moving to the country, individuals want to put an exclusive finishing touch to their properties. It has been a boost to crafts like mine.'

20

American and Danish buyers in particular are showing interest. 'Pricing,' he explains, 'depends on the intricacy of the design.' His most recent request was for a curly-coated dog. Whatever the occasion, Graham can create a gift with a difference.

A Graham has become increasingly busy, supplying flat-packed weathervanes to clients worldwide.

B Graham decided to concentrate his efforts on a weathervane business. He had served an apprenticeship as a precision engineer and had worked in that trade for 15 years when he and his wife, Liz, agreed to swap roles – she went out to work as an architectural assistant and he stayed at home to look after the children and build up the business.

C It's all a far cry from the traditional cockerel, the most common design for weathervanes.

D Last month, a local school was opened with his galleon ship weathervane hoisted above it.

E 'For centuries, weathervanes have kept communities in touch with the elements signalling those shifts in wind direction that bring about changes in the weather,' he explains.

F Graham has no plans for expansion, as he wants to keep the business as a rural craft.

G Graham has now perfected over 100 original designs. He works to very fine detail, always seeking approval for the design of the silhouette from the customer before proceeding with the hand-cutting.

Part 3

Read the following newspaper article and answer questions **21–26** on page **9**. On your answer sheet indicate the letter **A**, **B**, **C** or **D** against the number of each question.
Give only one answer to each question.

Indicate your answers **on the separate answer sheet**.

With the trees, I planted my stake in New Zealand

JONATHON PORRITT
TALKS TO
DANNY DANZIGER

Jonathon Porritt is the author of 'Seeing Green – The Politics of Ecology'.

I HAD a most peculiar period of my life when I didn't have any summers. I went out to New Zealand every summer here, which is the New Zealand winter, and so I had nine winters on the trot, which was great, because I like winter.

My parents came up with this idea of buying a small plot of land which 'the kids', my brother, sister and I, could look after. Mother said, 'If you can take the time and trouble to plant it with trees then you can have it.' The idea was that we would always have a stake in New Zealand, which is a lovely idea as my father was actually brought up there. And they found a plot of land about 20 miles north of Auckland in a place called Rangitoupuni. It's rather poor land, really, but it's quite good for planting trees on.

I've always been very keen and enthusiastic about land. I'd spent a year in Australia working on sheep stations and helping out in different farming jobs, and so the idea of planting trees sounded like a very nice idea, and I was immediately keen. I think the rest of the family got enthusiastic as we went along. I started planting in 1968, and by the end of 1972 between the three of us we'd planted the whole 70 acres.

In New Zealand in 1968 it was one of those winters. It rained an awful lot, endlessly in fact, and in a way it's idiotic to think back on it as such an immensely happy time as it rained pretty well most days that we were planting, and I don't suppose I've ever been wetter or colder for such a prolonged period.

There was a moment of truth every morning: getting ready for the next planting session. Coming out of the Land Rover relatively warm and dry, with the rain coming down, and your anorak still clammy from the day before, boots still sodden, hands fumbling with slippery laces.

'The brain begins to take over and to allow for all sorts of strange thoughts, ideas and reflections about life.'

In that first year I had a guy to work with me who was an experienced tree-planter, which was very helpful as I'd never planted trees seriously before all this. You have a planting bag around your neck which you fill with as many trees as you possibly can, and when your bag is full it's a nightmare, and it's only as it gets lighter that life gets easier.

In a way, the most difficult bit of the entire operation was getting the lines straight. You work out what spacing you're going to plant the trees at, and then you line up a series of three poles across as long a trajectory as you can get, and those poles then determine your lines. Once you're in line, you just plant all the way down the line till you get to the end, turn around and come back again. I enjoy hard physical work, and it certainly made me fit.

After a certain point you can plant trees almost on automatic, you become used to a rhythm, and you use the minimum number of spade strokes that you need to get the hole in the ground. The rhythm is something that everybody tells you about and, of course, it's true of many agricultural jobs that you actually have to train the body into a series of quite standardised moves, and then it becomes immensely easy: so you

develop an absolutely regular process of taking the tree out of the bag, digging a hole, putting it in the ground, stamping it in, and moving on. Mentally, it's very interesting. The brain begins to take over and to allow for all sorts of strange thoughts and ideas and reflections about life – a lot of my thinking about the natural world and our place in it, all of those things that have since dominated my life, first began to pop through my head in those days.

I've been back to New Zealand four times since then and watched the trees gradually grow, which has been very satisfying when you actually planted the things and you do then have a kind of stake in what happens and how they prosper.

I always dread reading in the newspapers stories of another high wind in New Zealand, or *Worst Drought Ever Hits New Zealand*. Such headlines make me feel extremely apprehensive. However, it worked out extremely well and those trees are now 20 years old, and in good fettle.

The only postscript I should add is that I took a term off from teaching, and I went back there in 1984, completely on my own for three months. And I wrote my first book there, *Seeing Green*. There's a little cabin on the tree farm which is fantastically basic, just a bed, a table and a chair. In the mornings I would do my writing; in the afternoons I would go off and prune the trees, and then do research in the evenings.

The connection between me and that area is still immensely strong. In many respects it's the place that I feel most closely identified with in terms of that link between people and the earth: it's a most powerful bond.

21   When the Porritts first considered buying a piece of land for their children to look after,

    A   Jonathon's brother and sister needed encouraging.
    B   Jonathon himself reacted positively.
    C   the whole family was equally enthusiastic.
    D   Jonathon's mother imposed unrealistic conditions.

22   When he started planting trees in 1968, Jonathon

    A   was employed by an expert tree-planter.
    B   had experience of the work in Australia.
    C   had only limited experience of tree-planting.
    D   had to learn from scratch how to do the job.

23   1968 was a happy time for Jonathon even though

    A   the work was physically demanding.
    B   he didn't like being separated from his family.
    C   the weather was very unpleasant.
    D   he didn't enjoy living alone.

24   When did Jonathon become efficient at planting trees?

    A   when he put fewer trees in his planting bag
    B   when he got used to the nature of the soil
    C   when he knew how to set up a planting line
    D   when he had become accustomed to the routine

25   Jonathon found planting trees to be

    A   the best way of keeping himself fit.
    B   an increasingly monotonous activity.
    C   a way to escape from reality.
    D   an opportunity to reflect on important issues.

26   What is Jonathon's present view of the place where he lived in New Zealand?

    A   He would like to spend more time there.
    B   He would like to write about it.
    C   He intends to return there soon.
    D   He has a strong commitment to it.

Part 4

Answer questions **27–42** by referring to the holiday brochure on pages **11–12**.

For questions **27–34**, answer by choosing from the holidays (**A–G**). Some of the choices may be required more than once. Indicate your answers **on the separate answer sheet.**

Note: When more than one answer is required, these may be given **in any order**.

You carry little with you.	**A** Wildlife and Natural History
27 .... **28**	
You may stay with local people.	**B** Ethnic Encounters
29 .... **30**	**C** Easy/Moderate Hiking
You need previous experience.	
31	**D** Major Treks
You are taught what is required.	**E** Wilderness Experience
32	
You visit places that few visitors see.	**F** Sailtreks/Seatreks
33 .... **34**	**G** Raft and River Journeys

For questions **35–42**, answer by choosing from the destinations (**A–H**). Some of the choices may be required more than once.

Note: When more than one answer is required, these may be given **in any order**.

You may stay on a boat.	**A** Nepal
35	**B** Uganda
You may leave the party for a short exploration.	
36 .... **37**	**C** the Dordogne River
You may be transported by experts.	**D** the Galapagos Islands
38	**E** the Alps
You may have your bags carried.	
39 .... **40** **41**	**F** Venezuela
You may travel by regular local transport.	**G** Zaire
42	**H** Thailand

Explore Worldwide
– small groups leave few footprints

Explore Worldwide is right in the forefront of adventure travel with trips designed for people who want to get more out of their holiday than just a beach. Our emphasis is on travel to new and unusual destinations, coupled with interesting and original itineraries. Our brochure contains over 100 original adventures – tours, treks, safaris and expeditions – in more than 60 countries around the world. Most trips last from 1–4 weeks.

Small Groups

Averaging 16 people. Small informal groups, expertly led. Giving you a real opportunity to discover more about the places we visit for yourself. More personal involvement brings you closer to the local scene and the local peoples. A stimulating experience for all travellers.

Different Modes of Travel

Many different kinds of transport are used. Often on the same trip. We travel by chartered coach or local bus, by train, expedition vehicle, minibus, boat, canoe, raft, camel, light plane etc. And often on foot. Each trip takes on the character of the local terrain.

Who Travels with *Explore*?

Interesting people with the resilience to tackle new situations and get the most out of an original adventure. Mainly from the UK, Europe, Australia, New Zealand, Canada and the States. All our trips are designed to be within the capabilities of almost anyone who enjoys good health, is reasonably fit, and above all adaptable. The majority are aged between 25 and 55. About half are couples. The rest are enterprising individuals travelling alone.

Activities and Interests

It's not easy to describe *Explore Worldwide*. Each trip is completely unique. So we have divided our worldwide adventures into 8 different categories, describing some of the main activities and interests. Each category represents a special highlight that is an integral part of a particular tour, and of course trips have several different highlights. However, please bear in mind that many other factors contribute to the success of all our trips as a whole. Unique places, unusual encounters, strange customs, unpredictable events, personal involvement – all play their part in the full enjoyment of your holiday.

Cultural/Adventure

Almost all the trips in our brochure have a strong cultural feeling. But a certain number of tours have this as their primary emphasis, focusing closely on local cultures, ethnic peoples and classic sites. For example, anyone looking for destinations of outstanding cultural and historical interest should consider our trips in **Egypt, Jordan, Syria, Yemen, Turkey, Greece, India, Bhutan, Thailand, China, Peru, Bolivia, Guatemala** and **Belize** – to mention a few of the places featured in our programme! Short day walks of 2–4 hours to visit unusual or off-the-tourist-track sites are often an integral part of our trips.

Wildlife and Natural History

Our wildlife safaris visit many of the world's greatest game parks and offer a thrilling encounter with animals in their natural state. Choose from dozens of remarkable destinations. In **Africa**, for example, you often have the freedom to step outside your safari vehicle and tackle the wild terrain for yourself. You could track the rare silver-back mountain gorilla in **Zaire**, go bush walking with tribal guides in **Uganda**, climb **Mount Kenya**, ride a canoe on the **Zambezi River** or a traditional *mokoro* in the **Okavango Delta**. Most African safaris camp, and full camping equipment is provided. A few offer hotel and lodge accommodation throughout. Elsewhere, in **Asia** and **South America**, on trips which include game viewing – say, our tiger safari in **India** – we usually stay in hotels, resthouses and jungle lodges. In Darwin's famous **Galapagos Islands** we live aboard a small motor yacht.

Ethnic Encounters

A special highlight of an *Explore Worldwide* adventure is the opportunity it offers to meet ethnic or tribal peoples. These could be the 'Blue Men' or Tuareg of the **Central Sahara**, the Maya of **Mexico**, or the colourful Huli of **Papua New Guinea**. Some, like the Bushmen of the **Kalahari Desert**, are nomadic wanderers. Others, like the pygmies of the **Ituri Forest**, are hunter-gatherers; or dry rice farmers like the friendly hilltribe peoples of **Northern Thailand**. Many are often part of an 'Old World' culture. Their societies are often under serious threat from unscrupulous exploiters. We travel in small groups only. Our aim is to help spread tolerance and understanding between different races and peoples, with the minimum of cultural and environmental disturbance.

Easy/Moderate Hiking

Many trips include a few days' easy walking through open countryside, based on tented or hotel accommodation; also village-to-village hiking which involves some trail walking with the prospect of overnighting along the way in private houses or basic village huts. You'll find such trips in **Spain's Sierra Nevada**, in **Provence, Tuscany, Crete, Corsica, Greece, Morocco, Turkey, Bulgaria,**

Thailand, Bhutan, Nepal, Venezuela, and many other *Explore Worldwide* destinations. On long distance walks involving more than one day, all your main luggage is transported by a separate vehicle, or carried by porters or pack animals. You simply bring a daypack for your personal gear.

Major Treks

A limited number of major treks are offered for strong mountain walkers. These sometimes involve walking at elevations over 10,000 feet, with substantial altitude gains and losses during a single day. We may lodge with the local people or rough-camp in the world's great mountain ranges like the **Atlas, Kackar, Himalayas** and **Andes**. Or we use a mixture of well-appointed camp-sites and alpine chalets in more sophisticated mountain areas such as the **Alps**. Such trips usually involve support vehicles, porterage or pack animals. We rarely backpack or carry heavy gear.

Wilderness Experience

Discovering one of the world's remote wilderness areas is a thrilling and memorable experience – perhaps the ultimate travel adventure. Such places have a strong fascination for the intrepid traveller, holding out the prospect of exotic new horizons. We explore the haunting beauty of the **Amazon Rainforest** and experience the powerful mystique of the **Sahara, Great Thar, Namib** and **Gobi Deserts**. They offer a chance to participate in an

adventure few people could ever dream of.

Sailtreks/Seatreks

These are among the most original and relaxing holidays in our brochure. We charter local boats and journey by traditional *felucca* sailboat through **Upper Egypt**; we utilise *gulets* (wooden motor yachts) in **Turkey** and island-to-island ferries in countries like **Greece** and **Thailand**. Our 2-masted schooner explores the islands of the **Indonesian Archipelago**, while a small motor yacht is chartered to cruise among the unique wildlife habitats of the **Galapagos**.

Raft and River Journeys

River journeys can last from a few hours to several days, and range from 2-person inflatables which participants paddle themselves (on the **Dordogne River**, for example) to all the fun, thrills and excitement of whitewater rafting navigated by skilled oarsmen (such as on Peru's beautiful **Urubamba River** or the wild **Trisuli River** in **Nepal**). No previous experience is necessary and the appropriate safety skills are quickly learned. Our river trips in **India, Africa** and the **Amazon** offer us a unique insight into the fertile margins and exotic jungles.

Get your free copy of the Explore Worldwide brochure NOW!

PAPER 2   WRITING (2 hours)

Part 1

You **must** answer this question.

1   A fortnight ago you were on holiday in Scotland. One evening you went to the cinema with a Scottish friend of yours, called Malcolm Taylor. On the way home together, you witnessed an attempt by a young man to steal a woman's handbag. Malcolm tried to help the woman and, although the thief managed to run away, nothing was stolen. Malcolm suffered a bad cut to his face. You have just received the letter below from Malcolm with the newspaper cutting on page **14** enclosed.

Read the letter and newspaper cutting and then, **using the information carefully**, write the **letter** and **note** listed on page **14**.

… It was great to see you last month. I'm glad you enjoyed your holiday – back at work now I suppose – hope it's not too boring! The reason I'm writing is to ask you a favour. If you read the enclosed, you'll see it's supposed to be a report about that incident outside the Rex Cinema; I'm sure you'll remember it. Anyway, as you can see, they've given the impression I was the mugger!! Whether it's just bad reporting or they've missed a paragraph I can't make out, but the facts are all wrong – even your nationality. Typical!

I've phoned them and they say they'll print a correction, but I know that just means a sentence hidden away at the bottom of one of the back pages.

Would you mind writing a letter to the paper, saying what really happened?

I think they'll print it if you've taken the trouble to write from abroad. I'd be really grateful – all my family's friends read this local paper and the report really makes me look bad.

Many thanks. Keep in touch, hope to see you again soon.

Malcolm

| EWENESS WEEKLY TIMES |
| Thursday May 27 2000 |

Handbag Thief Caught

A YOUNG MAN was arrested outside the Odeon Cinema in Grant Street last Thursday after attempting to snatch the handbag of a woman passer-by. Malcolm Taylor, 24, a Eweness resident, was accompanied by an American tourist who was not, however, involved in the incident. Miss Erskine, 27, suffered a cut to her face and was badly shaken. She said she was most upset by such an incident happening in a place like Eweness, but added 'I'm really most grateful to my rescuer.'

Now write:

(a) the **letter** to the 'Eweness Weekly Times' as requested by Malcolm (about 200 words)

(b) a relevant **note** to Malcolm (which you would attach to a copy of the letter) (about 50 words)

You must lay these out in an appropriate way but it is not necessary to include addresses.

Part 2

Choose **one** of the following writing tasks. Your answer should follow exactly the instructions given. Write approximately 250 words.

2   An English-speaking friend is going to stay in your home while you are on holiday. This is part of a letter which you receive from your friend.

> 'By the way, I hope I'll be able to watch TV while I'm staying at your flat. How does it work? How many channels will I be able to watch? What are the different channels like? Which programmes would you recommend me to watch? And are there any programmes which you think I should definitely avoid? Although I can't speak your language very well yet, I can understand quite a bit and I think I should improve a lot by watching while I'm staying in your place ...'

Write a **detailed note** which you leave in your home for your friend, covering all the points raised in the letter.

3 You have been asked to write an **article** for an international magazine about the status and care of the elderly.
Describe ways in which you think these have changed in your community over the past fifty years, and suggest developments you would like to see in the future.

Write your **article**.

4 This announcement has appeared in a local English language magazine.

Win a book token

   Which three books would you most like to take with you if you were going to live on a desert island?
   We are offering a prize for the best 250-word answer to this question.
   The books you write about can be in any language but your answer must be in English. You should include **clear** descriptions of the books and an explanation of **why** they would be of special importance for you.

Write your **entry** for the competition.

5 Your boss has received the following request from a local school and has asked you to respond. Write a suitable **report** covering all the points mentioned by the students.

We are a class of High School students doing a project on recruitment and in-service training in different parts of the world. We should be very grateful if you or a member of your staff could spare the time to supply us with a brief report on how your company recruits new staff and trains them, and on what training opportunities it offers to existing staff.

Write your **report**.

PAPER 3   ENGLISH IN USE (1 hour 30 minutes)

Part 1

For questions **1–15**, read the article below and then decide which word on page **17** best fits each space. Put the letter you choose for each question in the correct box on your answer sheet. The exercise begins with an example **(0)**.

Example:

0	A	0

THE BEGINNINGS OF FLIGHT

The story of man's mastery of the air is almost as old as man himself, a puzzle in which the essential **(0)** … were not found until a very late stage. However, to **(1)** … this we must first go back to the time when primitive man **(2)** … his food, and only birds and insects flew. We cannot know with any certainty when man first deliberately shaped weapons for throwing, but that **(3)** … of conscious design marked the first step on a road that **(4)** … from the spear and the arrow to the aeroplane and the giant rocket of the present **(5)** … . It would seem, in fact, that this **(6)** … to throw things is one of the most primitive and deep-seated of our instincts, **(7)** … in childhood and persisting into old age. The more mature ambition to throw things swiftly and accurately, which is the origin of most **(8)** … games, probably has its roots in the ages when the possession of a **(9)** … weapon and the ability to throw it with force and accuracy **(10)** … the difference between eating and starving.

It is significant that such weapons were **(11)** … and brought to their **(12)** … form at an early stage in history. If we were restricted to the same **(13)** … , it is doubtful if we could produce better bows and arrows than those that **(14)** … the armies of the past. The arrow was the first true weapon capable of maintaining direction over considerable **(15)** … . It was to be centuries before man himself could fly.

0	**(A)**	clues	**B**	keys	**C**	responses	**D**	resolutions
1	**A**	value	**B**	approve	**C**	understand	**D**	realize
2	**A**	pursued	**B**	hunted for	**C**	chased	**D**	followed up
3	**A**	act	**B**	deed	**C**	action	**D**	event
4	**A**	brings	**B**	moves	**C**	takes	**D**	leads
5	**A**	instant	**B**	day	**C**	hour	**D**	moment
6	**A**	feeling	**B**	urge	**C**	encouragement	**D**	emotion
7	**A**	coming	**B**	arriving	**C**	appearing	**D**	growing
8	**A**	exterior	**B**	outside	**C**	external	**D**	outdoor
9	**A**	suitable	**B**	fitting	**C**	related	**D**	chosen
10	**A**	involved	**B**	meant	**C**	told	**D**	showed
11	**A**	invented	**B**	imagined	**C**	planned	**D**	produced
12	**A**	last	**B**	older	**C**	latest	**D**	final
13	**A**	matters	**B**	substances	**C**	materials	**D**	sources
14	**A**	destroyed	**B**	ruined	**C**	spoiled	**D**	exploded
15	**A**	lengths	**B**	extents	**C**	areas	**D**	distances

Part 2

For questions **16–30**, complete the following article by writing each missing word in the correct box on your answer sheet. **Use only one word for each space.** The exercise begins with an example **(0)**.

Example:

0	having		0

EVOLUTION

It is generally accepted that present-day animals and plants differ from those of the past, **(0)** ... changed by a general process called evolution. But this theory has been widely accepted for little **(16)** ... than a hundred years. The present theory of evolution was developed **(17)** ... two naturalists – Charles Darwin and Alfred Russell Wallace – working independently.

   When he was a young man **(18)** ... 22, Darwin went as a naturalist on a round-the-world, map-making cruise aboard a British naval survey ship, *HMS Beagle*. The cruise began in 1831 and lasted **(19)** ... 1836. In the Galapagos Islands, Darwin came **(20)** ... a group of birds, later to become known **(21)** ... 'Darwin's finches'. They were similar to one **(22)** ... in their colour, song, nests and eggs, and were clearly descended **(23)** ... the same finch stock, **(24)** ... each had a different kind of beak and was adapted **(25)** ... a different way of life. **(26)** ... were seed-eaters, fly-catchers, woodpeckers and various other types.

   Darwin assumed that the ancestors of all **(27)** ... types had been blown to the islands in bleak weather, had survived and changed somehow **(28)** ... the various forms. In the years after the voyage, Darwin gradually came to the conclusion that individuals better suited to **(29)** ... environment would tend to leave more offspring while those **(30)** ... well adapted would die out.

Part 3

In **most** lines of the following text, there is **one** unnecessary word. It is either grammatically incorrect or does not fit in with the sense of the text. For each numbered line **31–46**, find this word and then write it in the box on your answer sheet. **Some lines are correct.** Indicate these lines with a tick (✔) in the box. The exercise begins with two examples **(0)** and **(00)**.

Example:

0	an	0
00	✔	0

DISCOVERY OF STAINLESS STEEL

0   Stainless steel was discovered by (an) accident in 1913 by the British

00 metallurgist Harry Brearley. He was experimenting with steel alloys –

31 combinations of metals – that they would be suitable for making gun

32 barrels. A few months later he had noticed that most of his rejected

33 specimens had rusted although one was containing 14 per cent

34 chromium had not. The discovery led to the development of stainless

35 steel. Ordinary steel goes rusts because it reacts easily with oxygen in

36 the air to produce crumbly red oxides. Other metals, such as aluminium,

37 nickel and chromium, also react in a much the same way but their oxides

38 form an impermeable surface layer, stopping oxygen to reacting with the

39 metal underneath. With Brearley's steel, the chromium formed such as

40 a film, protecting the metal from further attack, and the whole success of

41 stainless steel is based well on the fact that it has this one unique

42 advantage. In fact, a variety of stainless steels are now made. One

43 of the commonest contains of 18 per cent chromium and 8 per cent

44 nickel and is used for kitchen sinks. Kitchen knives are made of steel

45 containing about 13 per cent chromium. A very more corrosion-resistant

46 alloy is achieved by adding up an incredibly small amount of the metal

    molybdenum – these steels are used as cladding for buildings.

Part 4

For questions **47–61**, read the two texts on pages **20** and **21**. Use the words in the boxes to the right of the texts to form **one** word that fits in the same numbered space in the text. Write the new word in the correct box on your answer sheet. The exercise begins with an example **(0)**.

Example:

0	historic	0

TOURIST GUIDE

CAMBRIDGE MARKET

If you're visiting Cambridge, do go and see the **(0)** ... and **(47)** ... open market in the heart of the city. Fresh fruit, vegetables, meat and fish are for sale from 8.30am to 4.30pm **(48)** ... . But besides the fresh produce, you'll also find books, clothes, CDs and **(49)** ... , so there really is something for everyone. On Sundays there is a craft market which has gone through rapid **(50)** ... recently. Every stall has now been taken and there are currently over thirty stalls selling a wide range of goods from **(51)** ... by local artists to highly **(52)** ... jewellery and fashion ware. A recent addition has been a **(53)** ... stall selling shawls from Northern India, and this is proving extremely popular.

(0)	HISTORY
(47)	COLOUR
(48)	DAY
(49)	REFRESH
(50)	DEVELOP
(51)	PAINT
(52)	USUAL
(53)	FASCINATE

INFORMATION LEAFLET

HEALTHY DRIVING

Strange as it may seem, driving a car can cause many aches and pains. They only occur because drivers are **(54)** … about certain things and most are **(55)** … . For healthy driving:

- Keep your seat in a **(56)** … upright position.

- Always wear a seat belt and make sure the adjustment is correct. This also applies to children, who are put at risk by seat belts which are **(57)** … fitted.

- Don't set the headrest too low as this may cause serious **(58)** … in an accident.

- Relax as much as you can. If there's major traffic congestion, you could try **(59)** … up your shoulders and breathing **(60)** … .

- Avoid lifting weights when there's no **(61)** … to do so. Take care when moving heavy luggage and get help changing a tyre.

(54)	CARE
(55)	AVOID
(56)	REASON
(57)	CORRECT
(58)	INJURE
(59)	LOOSE
(60)	STEADY
(61)	NECESSARY

Part 5

For questions **62–74**, read the informal letter from a friend to a university student who wants to obtain a temporary summer job in a hospital. Use the information in it to complete the formal letter to the Personnel Officer of the hospital. The words you need **do not occur** in the informal letter. **Use no more than two words for each gap**. The exercise begins with an example **(0)**.

Example:

0	enquire	0
		_ _

LETTER FROM A FRIEND

> Dear Anita,
>
> Just a quick note to let you know that I've found out what you should do about getting a temporary job at the hospital.
>
> Write to the Personnel Officer; his name is Mr I. Cooper. Tell him that you're looking for a temporary summer job and that you're wondering whether they need anyone. Mention that I suggested you write to him – I know him fairly well. Of course, he knows me as Dr Ferguson.
>
> Tell him what you're doing now – you know, that you've been a student for about eighteen months – and that you'd really like to work in a hospital in your holiday because you've decided to become a hospital doctor when you get your degree.
>
> Since you haven't done that sort of work before, you'd better tell him that you really want to learn and that you'll take anything they offer you. It may mean being a general assistant on a ward – it's really hard work and there won't be much money in it, I'm afraid.
>
> I think you ought to put in your school certificates and your latest exam results from university because he'll probably want to see them. I wouldn't send the originals, though – you don't want them to get lost. And tell him that you'll send him any other info about yourself that he might want.
>
> Finish the letter off by telling him where he can get in touch with you – you'll be at that address until mid-June, won't you?
>
> Anyway, I must get back to work now.
>
> Love,
>
> James

LETTER TO PERSONNEL OFFICER

28, Highfield Place
Manchester

Mr I. Cooper
Personnel Officer
Archway Hospital   14 January 2000
Manchester

Tel: 936574

Dear Sir,

I am writing to **(0)** ... whether you have any **(62)** ... for temporary work. I have been **(63)** ... to write to you by Dr James Ferguson.

At **(64)** ... I am a second year student at university, taking a degree course **(65)** ... , and I would very **(66)** ... the opportunity to work in a hospital during my vacation, as it is my intention to become a hospital doctor when I **(67)** ... .

Although I have not as yet had any **(68)** ... this type of work, I am very keen to learn and would be willing to **(69)** ... any job you may be able to offer me. I would, for example, be quite prepared to work as a general ward assistant, although I realise it would not be very **(70)** ... .

I **(71)** ... photocopies of my school certificates and of my most **(72)** ... examination results at university. Should you require any further **(73)** ... , I will be happy to send them to you. I can be **(74)** ... until the middle of June at the above address and telephone number. I look forward to receiving your reply.

Yours faithfully

Anita Smithson

Part 6

For questions **75–80**, read the following text and then choose from the list **A–J** given below the best phrase to fill each of the spaces. Write one letter (**A–J**) in the correct box on your answer sheet. Each correct phrase may only be used once. **Some of the suggested answers do not fit at all.** The exercise begins with an example (**0**).

Example: | **0** | J | | **0** |

WHEN HOTELS OVERBOOK

Ann Marshall booked a room at the Granada Hotel in London. She wrote to confirm and specifically asked the hotel to hold her room 'all night' as she would be arriving very late. So as to emphasize the fact, the hotel highlighted in their confirmation letter **(0)** … . So when Mrs Marshall arrived at the hotel at 11 pm on the night, she was astonished **(75)** … . The staff arranged a room for her at another (inferior) hotel, and gave her £5 for taxi fares. Nevertheless, **(76)** … . She got to bed later and had **(77)** … . Above all, she didn't stay at the hotel of her choice. Hotels find themselves in something of a dilemma when demand for rooms is high, but they have rooms for guests **(78)** … . Some hotels may be tempted to let booked rooms and hope that 'no-shows' will see them through. Airlines do the same when selling tickets on scheduled flights.

You are normally entitled to damages for breach of contract if a hotel at which you have a firm booking, especially one which they've confirmed in writing, refuses a room **(79)** … . How much you're entitled to depends on the circumstances. The real point, though, is that if **(80)** … , those who run hotels and airlines might be less inclined to overbook.

A   she was expected to agree
B   she was very put out
C   to spend the night at a different hotel
D   when you arrive
E   who have not yet turned up
F   you take the trouble to complain
G   to be told it was full
H   to get up earlier than she intended
I   you do bother to book

J   that a late arrival was expected

PAPER 4   LISTENING (approximately 45 minutes)

Part 1

You will hear a news report about storm damage in three regions, the South West, the South East and the North. The effects of this damage are listed. For questions **1–18**, put a tick (✔) in the box to indicate what has happened in each region. If nothing has happened, put a cross (✘).

You will hear the recording **twice**.

		South West		*South East*		*North*
people trapped in cars	1		7		13	
people stranded at home	2		8		14	
animals in danger	3		9		15	
road or rail services affected	4		10		16	
electricity supplies affected	5		11		17	
reported fatalities	6		12		18	

Part 2

You will hear part of a telephone conversation in which a secretary is noting down details of an Open Day programme. For questions **19–25**, complete the notes.

Listen very carefully as you will hear the recording ONCE only.

9.30   Arrival

Welcomed by [   ] **19**

9.45   Introductory film; [   ] **20**

in staff lounge.

Followed by [   ] **21**

10.30 Tour of [   ] **22**

11.00 [   ] **23** : career structure

at AFG.

12.00 Visit to [   ] **24**

13.00 Lunch with [   ] **25**

14.00 Depart

Part 3

You will hear a radio interview with a young woman who runs her own restaurant. For questions **26–36**, complete the sentences.

You will hear the recording **twice**.

Christine Patterson started running her own restaurant | 26

In her first job she started work at | 27

She describes this as | 28

She often forgot whether or not she had remembered to add the | 29

However, she learnt the importance of doing things | 30

Christine's next job at 'The Gaiety' involved a lot of | 31

She realised she was an important part of a | 32

She learnt to work faster by | 33 | against other staff.

In her own restaurant, the new things she had to learn were how to manage | 34 | and | 35

It's her opinion that women in catering are not sufficiently good at | 36

Part 4

You will hear five short extracts in which people talk about various objects.

TASK ONE

For questions **37–41**, match the extracts as you hear them with the pictures labelled **A–H**.

A

B

| | 37 |

C

D

| | 38 |

E

F

| | 39 |

G

H

| | 40 |

| | 41 |

TASK TWO

For questions **42–46**, match the extracts as you hear them with the purposes listed **A–H**.

What is the purpose of the conversation?

A apologising for a mistake

B complaining about something

C describing something

D explaining what he/she wants

E expressing approval of something

F checking something is suitable

G making a promise

H seeking help with a problem

conversation 1 | | 42 |

conversation 2 | | 43 |

conversation 3 | | 44 |

conversation 4 | | 45 |

conversation 5 | | 46 |

Remember that you must complete both tasks as you listen. You will hear the recording twice.

PAPER 5   SPEAKING (15 minutes)

There are two examiners. One (the interlocutor) conducts the test, providing you with the necessary materials and explaining what you have to do. The other examiner (the assessor) will be introduced to you, but then takes no further part in the interaction.

Part 1 (3 minutes)

The interlocutor will first ask you and your partner a few questions. You will then be asked to find out some information about each other, on topics such as hobbies, interests, career plans, etc.

Part 2 (4 minutes)

You will each be given the opportunity to talk for about a minute, and to comment briefly after your partner has spoken.

   The interlocutor gives you a set of pictures and asks you to talk about them for about one minute. Each set of pictures has a different focus, so it is important to listen carefully to the interlocutor's instructions. The interlocutor then asks your partner a question about your pictures and your partner responds briefly.

   You will then be given another set of pictures to look at. Your partner talks about these pictures for about one minute. This time the interlocutor asks you a question about your partner's pictures and you respond briefly.

Part 3 (4 minutes)

In this part of the test you and your partner will be asked to talk together. The interlocutor will place a new set of pictures on the table between you. This stimulus provides the basis for a discussion. The interlocutor will explain what you have to do.

Part 4 (4 minutes)

The interlocutor will ask some further questions, which will lead to a more general discussion of what you have talked about in Part 3. You will be encouraged to comment on what your partner says, and the interlocutor will also take part in the discussion.

Test 2

PAPER 1   READING (1 hour 15 minutes)

Part 1

Answer questions **1–14** by referring to the magazine article about handwriting on page **31**.

For questions **1–14**, answer by choosing from the handwriting characteristics (**A–I**). Some of the choices may be required more than once. Indicate your answers **on the separate answer sheet**.

1 a person who has recently had a shock	**A** writing that is not joined together
2 a person who dislikes company	
3 a person who cannot be trusted	**B** writing that ignores the accepted rules
4 a person who is not lively	
5 a secretive person	**C** writing that has not been done firmly
6 a person who has committed a crime	
7 an honest person	**D** writing that is well-formed
8 a selfish person	
9 a confident person	**E** unusually large letters
10 an emotional person	
11 a person with a medical problem	**F** a signature that has changed
12 a person of high intelligence	
13 a person with creative talent	**G** letters that are not formed separately
14 an emotionally immature person	
	H writing with a lot of capitals
	I writing like that of a child

1 ....   6 ....   11 ....
2 ....   7 ....   12 ....
3 ....   8 ....   13 ....
4 ....   9 ....   14 ....
5 ....   10 ....

The pen is mightier than the psychoanalyst
The study of handwriting to reveal a person's character is gaining support

If you applied for a job in some countries, you would almost certainly be asked for a sample of your handwriting. And it would be the handwriting, as much as anything else, that would determine your suitability for the job.

Handwriting analysis, or graphology, is accepted as a genuine science in many countries. Researchers say it can be a useful tool in indicating certain illnesses, such as heart disease and cancer, and can reveal psychological states and emotional disturbances.

Handwriting analysis is increasingly being used for vocational guidance and as an adjunct to interviews. Many big companies now employ graphologists to analyse the handwriting of potential candidates for key jobs.

But most doctors and psychiatrists remain dubious about the value of graphology. Patricia Marne, a professional graphologist for more than 20 years, argues that they should take it more seriously. She believes that handwriting can indicate psychological characteristics as well as certain medical conditions.

She says: 'Handwriting is a powerful indicator of social class and intelligence. But more than that, it can be used to assess mental ability and potential, whether a person should concentrate on arts or sciences, and whether they have a devious or open character.'

According to Ms Marne, graphology can be particularly useful in assessing possible criminal tendencies: 'Criminals all have disturbed handwriting, mostly illiterate and poorly-shaped. Most criminals come from deprived backgrounds and have arrested emotional development. This often shows up in unusually childish handwriting and in going over letters several times.

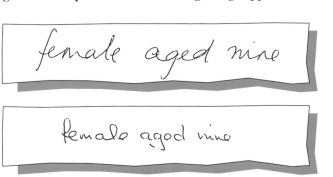

The person behind the handwriting: examples analysed by graphologist Patricia Marne. 'I can tell whether people are honest, manipulators, or reliable employees.'

'Young male offenders frequently have very high ascenders, indicating that they live in a world of fantasy and dream of making it big. Graphologists can tell whether violence is about to erupt, whether the writer is under unbearable pressure, and whether there are psychopathic tendencies. Handwriting can be used to predict would-be suicides.'

Heart and lung problems can also show up, she says. 'You can't make a diagnosis from one sample, unless the writing is obviously shaky or disturbed. But if over a period of time it changes or becomes disjointed, if there's a break in the signature which did not exist previously, that could be a sign that something quite serious has occurred.'

A severe emotional upset can also show up in a temporarily altered signature, she maintains.

Ms Marne says handwriting can be used to reveal other psychological characteristics. People with writing in which letters form 'threads' instead of being individually formed are, apparently, devious and clever. Those who write mainly in capitals are trying to conceal their true selves from others. Very light pressure indicates sensitivity and lack of vitality. Originality in handwriting – how far the writer has deviated from copybook script – indicates confidence and artistic ability. Disconnected writing is the cardinal sign of the loner.

Very small signatures indicate inhibition and an inferiority complex; circles over the 'i' are a bid for attention, and crossing the 't' heavily over the whole word is a sign of intolerance and a patronising attitude.

Ms Marne says it takes six years of study and experience to be able to analyse handwriting accurately, and this has to be combined with empathy and intuition. She feels that more research is needed to put graphology on a proper scientific footing.

This will happen soon, she believes. 'It's actually far more accurate than psychoanalysis, as you can tell the whole history of the person, including all their emotional crises, without asking them questions to which they may give wrong answers.'

Interesting as all this may sound, there is little hard evidence to support such claims. Some psychiatrists are highly critical of them. Handwriting, they say, is a product of education, artistic ability and the type of writing taught – and has no other significance.

Part 2

For questions **15–20**, choose which of the paragraphs **A–G** on page **33** fit into the numbered gaps in the magazine article below. There is one extra paragraph, which does not fit in any of the gaps.

Indicate your answers **on the separate answer sheet**.

A trumpet isn't just for Christmas ...

It is strange how many musicians, even leading ones, come from homes without music. Out of the blue, Hakan Hardenberger, the only son of totally unmusical parents in a country district of southern Sweden, has at the age of 30 established himself as unique among the world's trumpet-players today.

15

Recently in one of London's premier concert halls he played the Hummel Trumpet Concerto, something of a party-piece for him, while on television a whole feature was devoted to his work and development, filmed both here and in Sweden.

Born near Malmo, he owes his career to the accident of a Christmas present when he was only eight.

16

The success of the gift was instant. The boy never stopped playing. His mother managed to contact the second trumpet-player in the Malmo Symphony Orchestra, whom she persuaded to give her son lessons.

17

There the mature Hardenberger has to draw a line between himself and his teacher. 'The trumpet is so primitive an instrument,' he explains, 'that you can't build a trumpet that is acoustically perfect. Whatever you do, it will have imperfections. Besides, you can't find two mouthpieces exactly the same. To me it is a matter of getting to know the imperfections and making a relationship with them.'

18

And unlike the great British contender among virtuoso trumpet-players, John Wallace, who developed originally from a brass-band background and then through working in orchestras, Hardenberger has always thought of himself as a solo artist pure and simple.

19

His parents gave him every chance to practise, and went along with his ambition to make trumpet-playing a career. It was then a question of where, at 15, he should be sent to study. America, Bo Nilsson's first choice, was thought to be too far away and too dangerous, which meant that he went instead at the age of 16 to study in Paris with Pierre Thibaud. Thibaud confirmed his prejudice against going into an orchestra, saying that 'Playing in the orchestra is like digging in the garden.'

20

Thibaud suggested that he should enter the competition 'just for experience'. Hardenberger learned the pieces for the first round only, but he won through to the second. Luckily he already knew most of the pieces in that round too, but on getting through to the final he was faced with a concerto that had already daunted him. He didn't win first prize that time, but he enjoyed the performance, realising that though he 'played like a pig', people did listen to him.

Quoted like that, Hardenberger's realism about his work and his career may sound arrogant, but that would be a totally false impression. Thoughtfully he refuses to try and analyse what such a gift of communication might consist of, as 'You risk destroying it in trying to explain. The power of the music lies in the fact that it can always move people.'

A From the very start Hardenberger seems to have had the gift of finding the right compromise, and making that relationship. Without any sense of boasting, he explains that even in his boyhood years the characteristic Hardenberger sound was already recognisable, 'the first thing I acquired'.

B He is always anxious to extend his repertory. Hans-Werner Henze is the latest composer to be writing a piece for him, while on other records he has unearthed rare works from the 17th and 18th centuries.

C He was objective enough about himself to know that he played the trumpet better than others of his age, but it was only at the end of the first competition he entered, at the age of 17 during his first year in Paris, that he came to realise that in addition he had a particular gift of communicating.

D His father, unmusical but liking Louis Armstrong's playing, had the idea of giving his only son a trumpet. Being a serious man, he didn't pick a toy trumpet, but took advice and bought a genuine grown-up instrument.

E His records are continually opening up new repertory, not just concertos by long-neglected composers of the baroque and classical periods, but new works too. When you meet him, bright-eyed and good-looking, he seems even younger than his years, as fresh and open in his manner as the sound of the trumpet.

F Bo Nilsson was an up-and-coming musician, and at once spotted natural talent. Hardenberger consistently blesses his luck to have got such a teacher right from the start, one who was himself so obsessed with the trumpet and trumpet-playing that he would search out and contact players all over the world, and as a 'trumpet fanatic' was 'always looking for another mouthpiece'.

G From early boyhood he had as a role-model the French trumpeter, Maurice André, another player who bypassed the orchestra. The boy bought all his records, and idolised him.

Part 3

Read the following newspaper article and answer questions **21–25** on page **35**. On your answer sheet, indicate the letter **A**, **B**, **C** or **D** against the number of each question. Give only one answer to each question.

Indicate your answers **on the separate answer sheet**.

Hit and miss of mass marketing

AS ALMOST everyone knows, advertising is in the doldrums. It isn't just the recession. Advertising started to plummet early in 1989, well before the recession really began to bite.

Advertising's problems are more fundamental, and the decline is worldwide. The unhappy truth is that advertising has failed to keep up with the pace of economic change.

Advertisers like to think in terms of mass markets and mass media; but as brands and media have proliferated, target markets have fragmented. Even campaigns for major brands ought to be targeted at minority audiences, but they rarely are. That is the principal way in which advertising has gone astray.

Think about your own shopping habits. If you visit a supermarket you may leave with 30, 40 or perhaps 50 items listed on your checkout bill, the average number of items of all kinds purchased per visit of all kinds.

Many of these will not be advertised brands; some others will be multiple purchases of the same brand. At a maximum you will have bought a handful of advertised brands from the 15,000 lines on sale in the store. Over a year you are unlikely to buy more than a few hundred brands.

Consumer durables? Perhaps a dozen a year. Cars? If yours is a new car, the statistical likelihood is that it is supplied by your employer.

If it isn't, you only buy one every three years. And though it may seem otherwise, you do not buy that many clothes either, and most of them will not be advertised brands.

Even when you throw in confectionery, medicines, hardware, all the services you can think of, it is virtually certain you do not buy more than 400 different brands a year. Compare that figure with the 32,500 branded goods and services that, according to Media Register, are advertised. Let's ignore the 23,000 which spend less than £50,000 a year, and concentrate on the 9,500 brands that Media Register individually lists and analyses.

Mr and Mrs Average have bought 400 of that 9,500, and not all because of their advertising. That's about 4 per cent. So you can forget that naive claim usually attributed to Lord Leverhulme: 'Half of my advertising is wasted but I've no way of knowing which half.' You could say that 96 per cent of all advertising is wasted, but nobody knows which 96 per cent.

When you're watching TV tonight, count how many of the commercials are for brands you buy or are likely to buy in the future. For most people the figure seems to be about one in 16 (6 per cent) so the commercials for the other 15 (94 per cent) are, on the face of it, wasted.

You probably think you're a

special case, that you are impervious to advertising. Almost everyone thinks the same. But you aren't and they aren't. The truth is nobody buys most of the brands they see advertised.

Waste is inherent in the use of media for advertising. The notion that every reader of a publication or every viewer of a commercial break might immediately rush out and buy all or even many of the brands advertised is ludicrous. People register only a tiny number of advertisements they see and ignore the rest, so waste cannot be avoided. That does not mean advertising isn't cost-effective. Millions of advertisements have proved it is.

Advertising has to communicate with large numbers of people to reach the relevant minority, because the advertiser cannot know, in advance, exactly which individuals will respond to his blandishments. Media advertising works, despite its much publicised expense, because it is a cheap means of mass communication.

Nonetheless, all waste is gruesome. With smart targeting the advertiser can minimise the wastage by increasing the *percentage* of readers or viewers who will respond; but he can never know *precisely* who will respond. Even the most accurate and finely tuned direct mail-shot never achieves a 100 per cent response. This is one of the fundamental differences between the use of media and face-to-face selling. It is possible, just, to envisage a salesman scoring with every prospective client he speaks to. The same could never happen when media are used. If the advertiser knew exactly which people were going to respond there would be no point in using media at all. The advertiser could communicate with them directly.

This is as true of Birth, Marriage and Death notices as it is of soft drink commercials. Any advertiser who can net one million new customers (2 per cent of the adult population) is doing well. Of soap powder, the two top-selling brands in supermarkets would be delighted with a million extra customers. So that any advertising campaign, for any product (or any political party for that matter) which could win over 2 per cent of the population would be outstandingly successful: and that, as I began by saying, is but a tiny minority of the population.

The most cost-effective way to reach them may be the use of mass media, but if advertising is to get going again its message will need to be more tightly targeted than ever before.

---

21 How can advertisers cut down on waste?
  A by using more face-to-face, direct selling techniques
  B by advertising through the mail rather than on TV
  C by aiming their advertising at particular groups of consumers
  D by using mass media advertising for certain types of products only

22 Advertising seems to be effective for
  A about half of all products.
  B many well-known brands.
  C very few products.
  D the most heavily advertised products.

23 Advertising through TV and other media is considered worthwhile because
  A a huge number of people see the adverts.
  B consumers are influenced far more than they realise.
  C it is easy to target a specialised audience.
  D people respond immediately to TV advertising.

24 One of the advertising industry's problems is that
  A manufacturers are not spending enough on their campaigns.
  B there are too many good quality products on the market.
  C nowadays consumers have less money to spend.
  D marketing is not sufficiently well-directed.

25 In order to be successful, advertisers need to
  A research carefully who is most likely to buy the product.
  B achieve only a small percentage increase in sales.
  C consider which type of advertising will be most effective.
  D target the widest possible audience among the adult population.

Part 4

Answer questions **26–41** by referring to the article about apples on pages **37–38**.

For questions **26–34**, answer by choosing from the list of apples (**A–G**). Some of the choices may be required more than once. Indicate your answers **on the separate answer sheet**.

Which apple

26 got its name because it looked like another fruit?

27 was a very small size?

28 was a Roman apple suited to the English climate?

29 gave its name to a trade?

30 contributed to the development of a new cultivation system?

31 was used as a cooking apple for centuries?

32 was found growing among things that had been thrown away?

33 had its name changed as a result of an appreciative comment?

34 was different in colour from earlier apples?

A wilding

B Decio

C Pearmain

D Costard

E Pippin

F Delicious

G Granny Smith

For questions **35–41**, answer by choosing from the list of people (**A–G**). Some of the choices may be required more than once.

Who

35 returned from a successful mission abroad?

36 was the subject of many stories?

37 noticed something strange about a dead tree?

38 sent a representative to learn about growing techniques abroad?

39 became the provider for the family?

40 valued apple-pips very highly?

41 explained the development of a particular apple in religious terms?

A Romans

B Henry VIII

C Richard Harris

D settlers

E John Chapman

F Jesse Hiatt

G Maria Anne Smith

A history of the apple

Apples have been with us since the dawn of recorded time, in countless varieties of colour, shape and size. But the late twentieth century is in danger of squandering its heritage.

Prehistoric wilding 8,000 BC

Human beings have been munching apples since prehistoric times. They spat out apple-pips in neolithic Britain. And 10,000 years ago they left apple remains to carbonise around their Swiss and Italian lakeside homes. In Switzerland and in the regions adjoining the Caucasus mountains, ancient humans even appear to have dry-stored apple-halves for winter. But these were wild crab apples, tiny wizened fruit which, in Ancient Britain, came to be known as 'wildings'. They had little in common with the apples we know today.

Norman knowledge 1000 AD

From the Romans the French learned great fruit-growing skills which were developed in the monasteries. This knowledge, which included expert cider-making, was taken to Britain from Roman times, like the dessert apple, Decio – thought to have been introduced by the Roman general, Etio. But most Roman varieties were unsuitable for the British climate and the Norman varieties rapidly took precedence. British monks continued experimenting and developing new apples, and it is from these varieties that Western apples are largely descended.

Mediaeval favourites 1200

Several kinds of apples became established in Britain during the thirteenth century. The Old English Pearmain, recorded in 1204 and so named because of its pear-like shape, was the main dessert apple until well into the eighteenth century. Its cooking partner was the Costard, which was sold in the markets of Oxford from 1296 until the end of the seventeenth century and gave us the word 'costermonger' – meaning someone who sells fruit and vegetables in the street. But prosperity declined as the country was hit by successive droughts, the Black Death and the Wars of the Roses. Fewer apples were produced and more were imported. This went on until the sixteenth century when Henry VIII ordered his chief fruiterer, Richard Harris, to visit France and learn about apple cultivation. Harris returned with a 'great store of grafts' including the famous Pippins, from which he grew the first ever modern-style orchard at Teynham in Kent.

Settler treasure 1750

By the seventeenth century apples were so popular in Britain that the first settlers who sailed to Canada, Australia, the US, South Africa and New Zealand took apples and apple-pips with them, counting these among their most treasured possessions. Captain Bligh of the Bounty took the first apples to Australia; Jan van Riebeeck, the founder of Cape Settlement, took them to South Africa and the Pilgrim Fathers who boarded the Mayflower carried them to America. In North America the most famous apple-planter was John Chapman, or 'Johnny Appleseed'. Born in 1774, he planted seedling nurseries from Pennsylvania in the

east through Ohio into Indiana in the west. The Indians regarded him as a medicine man and his apple-tree enthusiasm, odd clothing and religious devotion – he distributed religious tracts torn in parts for widespread circulation – started many folktales. He was said, for example, to be so kind to God's creatures that he even slept with bears.

Modern Delicious 1850

About this time in Iowa, a Quaker farmer called Jesse Hiatt discovered something sprouting from the roots of a dead tree. The shoot grew into an apple tree bearing a totally new apple which Hiatt named 'Hawkey'. He sent it to a fruit show and on biting into one the judge exclaimed 'Delicious, delicious!'. In 1895 the apple was introduced to the trade as a 'Delicious' and became one of the most widely grown apples in the world.

Granny Smith 1850

Another of the most famous modern apples was discovered in Australia by Maria Anne Smith. The daughter of transported convicts, Maria was fiercely independent, rejecting both the criminal life of her parents and the bureaucratic hypocrisy of the colonial administration. She worked as a midwife in the small township of Eastwood in New South Wales, where she was known as 'Granny-Smith' because she took on responsibility for maintaining the farm and orchard, which was the family's main source of income. One day in 1868 she found a small tree pushing its way through a pile of discarded fruit. She transplanted it and before long was harvesting the world's first major crop of green apples, soon to be famous all over the world. When asked how the tree came about she said, 'Well, it's just like God to make something useful out of what we think is rubbish' – a comment which referred not only to the fruit but also her own convict origins.

Uniformity rules 1950

Apples are now grown all over the world from Himachal Pradesh in northern India to small luxury orchards throughout Africa. Most, though, are grown commercially and come from just half a dozen varieties – usually chosen for their red skin or because they travel well rather than because they taste good. A plague of uniformity is sweeping the world, numbing the taste-buds and reducing the gene pool. While amateur gardeners in the UK have kept many old apple varieties alive, the US has lost forever most of the apples it had 100 years ago.

But consumers are starting to demand more variety. We can't leave the responsibility of saving diversity in our apples – or any other food – up to the random selections of amateur gardeners. We must insist on a world where natural diversity is valued and protected for the benefit of all.

PAPER 2   WRITING (2 hours)

Part 1

You **must** answer this question.

1   You are studying English at a local institute of education. As part of your course you have to do a special project on some aspect of the English language. One day you receive three notes related to your project.

Read the notes below carefully and then, **using the information given**, write the postcard, note and letter described on page **40**.

Can I just remind all my students who have chosen the special project on 'Varieties of English Around the World' that they should be giving that piece of work to me by the end of this month? I would like to keep strictly to this deadline, so remember, you have only about 4 weeks left!

    J.R.K.

THE ENGLISH LIBRARY

We regret to inform you that we have been unable to locate a copy of:

The English Spoken in India
Author: V. J. SINGH

It is possible for us to make further enquiries through the inter-library loans system, but as this may well take 6 to 9 weeks, we would ask you to confirm that you would like us to proceed.

How's your project on the English spoken in India going? Sounds interesting, even if you are finding the research a little hard to do. Maybe I can help. It occurs to me that books may not be all you need! I have a terribly intellectual aunt who's a great traveller, and takes a keen interest in all kinds of aspects of the places she's been to. She was actually born in India, and I think, if you ask her nicely, she'll be able to give you all kinds of examples of how English is used there. She could certainly tell you about words and idioms which are only used in India, and about things like pronunciation and any differences in grammar. In fact, I can mention it to her myself, but I think you should write her a letter, telling her what you're doing, and asking her if she can give you some details and examples. Don't forget to tell her you're an old friend of mine! She's called Kumari Patel (perhaps you'd better call her Dr Patel!) and her address is 32 John St, Newhall, Cheshire.

All the best

Meena

Now write:

(a) a **postcard** to the English Library (about 50 words)

(b) a **note** to Meena (about 50 words)

(c) a **letter** to Dr Patel (about 150 words)

You do not need to use postal addresses.

Part 2

Choose **one** of the following writing tasks. Your answer should follow exactly the instructions given. Write approximately 250 words.

2   This is part of a letter that you receive from a friend.

> 'As you know, I finish school this summer and I'm looking forward to starting work and earning some money of my own. Eventually I want to open my own shop and intend to get a job in the local department store straightaway to gain as much practical experience as possible. Of course my parents want me to go to college and do a business course but I feel I'd learn more on the job. My brother suggests I spend a year travelling before I make up my mind – so I could even go to Australia or somewhere and improve my English. Please let me know what you think ...'

Write to your friend, giving **practical advice**, referring to the points in the letter.

3   You have been asked by a college magazine to write an **article** entitled 'How to enjoy yourself without spending a fortune'.
You should describe a range of free or inexpensive activities available in your town, recommending those activities which you personally feel are best suited to new students.

Write your **article**.

4   An English friend is going to stay in your flat while you are away. You have always helped your elderly next-door neighbour, who can be rather difficult. You would like your friend to continue helping him/her during your absence. Write some **notes** to leave for your friend, giving particular information and advice on how to deal with the neighbour.

Write your **notes**.

5   You have just seen the following advertisement.

ARE YOU HIGHLY RESPONSIBLE & RESOURCEFUL?

Individual or couple required to live in our beautiful house in the English countryside, large gardens, swimming pool etc. for three months.
We shall be abroad on business and you will have to supervise painters and decorators, keep the gardens tidy and deal with phone calls.
To live in luxury, rent-free, write giving details of why we should entrust our house to you, with the names of two referees, to

P.O. Box 423, Rainton, Hants.

Write your **application** for this position giving relevant information about yourself.

PAPER 3 ENGLISH IN USE (1 hour 30 minutes)

Part 1

For questions **1–15**, read the article below and then decide which word on page **43** best fits each space. Put the letter you choose for each question in the correct box on your answer sheet. The exercise begins with an example **(0)**.

Example:

THE LANGUAGE OF TEARS

The ability to weep is a uniquely human form of emotional response. Some scientists have suggested that human tears are **(0)** … of an aquatic past – but this does not seem very likely. We cry from the moment we enter this **(1)** … , for a number of reasons. Helpless babies cry to **(2)** … their parents that they are ill, hungry or uncomfortable. As they **(3)** … they will also cry just to attract parental attention and will often stop when they get it.

The idea that **(4)** … a good cry can do you **(5)** … is a very old one and now it has scientific **(6)** … since recent research into tears has shown that they **(7)** … a natural painkiller called enkaphalin. By **(8)** … sorrow and pain this chemical helps you to feel better. Weeping can increase the quantities of enkaphalin you **(9)** … .

Unfortunately, in our society we impose restrictions upon this naturally **(10)** … activity. Because some people still regard it as a **(11)** … of weakness in men, boys in particular are admonished when they cry. This kind of repression can only increase stress, both emotionally and physically.

Tears of emotion also help the body **(12)** … itself of toxic chemical **(13)** … , for there is more protein in them than in tears resulting from cold winds or other irritants. Crying comforts, calms and can be very enjoyable – **(14)** … the popularity of the highly emotional films which are commonly **(15)** … 'weepies'. It seems that people enjoy crying together almost as much as laughing together.

0	**A**	witness	**B**	evidence	**C**	result	**D**	display
1	**A**	world	**B**	place	**C**	earth	**D**	space
2	**A**	communicate	**B**	persuade	**C**	inform	**D**	demonstrate
3	**A**	evolve	**B**	change	**C**	develop	**D**	alter
4	**A**	doing	**B**	making	**C**	getting	**D**	having
5	**A**	better	**B**	fine	**C**	good	**D**	well
6	**A**	validity	**B**	truth	**C**	reality	**D**	reason
7	**A**	contain	**B**	retain	**C**	hold	**D**	keep
8	**A**	struggling	**B**	fighting	**C**	opposing	**D**	striking
9	**A**	construct	**B**	achieve	**C**	provide	**D**	produce
10	**A**	curing	**B**	treating	**C**	healing	**D**	improving
11	**A**	hint	**B**	symbol	**C**	feature	**D**	sign
12	**A**	release	**B**	rid	**C**	loosen	**D**	expel
13	**A**	rubbish	**B**	waste	**C**	leftovers	**D**	remains
14	**A**	consider	**B**	remark	**C**	distinguish	**D**	regard
15	**A**	named	**B**	entitled	**C**	subtitled	**D**	called

Part 2

For questions **16–30**, complete the following article by writing each missing word in the correct box on your answer sheet. **Use only one word for each space**. The exercise begins with an example **(0)**.

Example: | 0 | like | | 0 |

ROBOTS

The popular idea of a robot is a machine that acts **(0)** … and resembles a human being. But the robots that are increasingly **(16)** … used for a wide range of tasks do not look human-like **(17)** … all. The robots **(18)** … work in car factory production lines look something like cranes. The mobile robots used **(19)** … army bomb-disposal squads look like wheelbarrows on tracks. And children **(20)** … likened a mobile robot used in school to teach **(21)** … computer programming to a giant sweet. Robots **(22)** … , however, resemble human beings in the range of actions that they can carry out. Instead of repeatedly performing **(23)** … one action, like an automatic machine, a robot can perform **(24)** … chain of different actions. Its movements are controlled **(25)** … by oil or air pressure or by electric motors, and its brain is a small computer that directs its movements. Inside the computer's memory **(26)** … the instructions **(27)** … carrying out a task – picking chocolates from a container and putting them in the right part of a display box, for example. By changing the programme, the robot can **(28)** … made to vary the task, or do **(29)** … different within the limits of the activities it is designed **(30)** … .

Part 3

In **most** lines of the following text, there is **one** unnecessary word. It is either grammatically incorrect or does not fit in with the sense of the text. For each numbered line **31–46**, find this word and then write it in the box on your answer sheet. **Some lines are correct.** Indicate these lines with a tick (✔) in the box. The exercise begins with two examples **(0)** and **(00)**.

Examples:

0	the	0
00	✔	0

WANTED

0   'Wanted' ran a small ad in The Times. 'Assistant for the famous cookery

00 writer. Three-month contract – £400.' The ad was answered by a young

31 woman, recently widowed and with a small baby, desperate for a work

32 of any kind. The hours were long and £400 seemed very little for three

33 months' of employment. But she was absolutely desperate and she got

34 the job. It proved harder than she had been anticipated, as the famous

35 writer proved as tyrannical, ungrateful and a slave driver. The first week

36 of helping to him was almost more than the young woman felt she could

37 stand. Only did the thought of the bread that she was putting in her

38 baby's mouth prevented her leaving from the job. At the end of the first

39 week, she was given a lift at home by the cookery writer's secretary. On

40 the way she confided how desperately she had needed the job and

41 admitted just how welcome even the miserable £400 was mentioned in

42 the advertisement would be. The secretary gave her such an odd look

43 that the young woman asked what it the matter was. 'I don't think you

44 quite understand,' answered the secretary. 'It's you who has to pay

45 for him £400.' At first the young woman was silent. She was temporarily

46 lost for some words, but then she began to laugh, and she laughed until

the tears poured down her cheeks.

Part 4

For questions **47–61**, read the two texts on pages **46** and **47**. Use the words in the boxes to the right of the texts to form **one** word that fits in the same numbered space in the text. Write the new word in the correct box on your answer sheet. The exercise begins with an example **(0)**.

Example:

0	involvement	0

JOB ADVERTISEMENT

Total initiative

   Total (0) ...

      Total (47) ...

Experienced Personal Assistant for Senior Global Vice President.
We're one of the world's most **(48)** ... companies. We employ over
120,000 people who all enjoy working our way. We free you to
achieve your **(49)** ... in the way that suits you best.
Our Senior Vice President has a very **(50)** ... schedule to meet.
We need you to organise her diary and run the office, to give her
the **(51)** ... to focus on key strategic business issues.
The work is challenging, involving you in reacting **(52)** ... to
incoming business and organising meetings and **(53)** ... . You'll
need to be capable of working at a senior level, and have
exceptional telephone skills and be a good all-round
communicator.

(0)	INVOLVE
(47)	LOYAL
(48)	SUCCEED
(49)	OBJECT
(50)	DEMAND
(51)	FREE
(52)	RAPID
(53)	CONFER

MAGAZINE ARTICLE

TAKE A DEEP BREATH

Since this time yesterday, you've breathed in and out approximately 20,000 times. Over a lifetime you'll take in more than a hundred million breaths. And, like every other living **(54)** … , you will have taken them completely **(55)** … . Our lives are **(56)** … on breathing, but, even so, most of us do it **(57)** … .

To see the best, really **(58)** … breathing, watch how a baby's stomach rises and falls. It's extremely **(59)** … to see poor breathing among children, but by the time most reach secondary school, they're breathing in a shallow and restricted way.

According to American **(60)** … , poor breathing plays a role in seventy-five per cent of health problems. Their **(61)** … show that correct breathing increases your oxygen intake and the efficiency of your body. This makes energy levels rise and stress levels fall.

(54)	CREATE
(55)	INSTINCT
(56)	DEPEND
(57)	APPROPRIATE
(58)	HEALTH
(59)	COMMON
(60)	RESEARCH
(61)	INVESTIGATE

Part 5

For questions **62–74**, read the notes made about a museum inspection and use the information to complete the formal letter to the head of the museum. The words you need **do not occur** in the notes. **Use no more than two words for each gap**. The exercise begins with an example **(0)**.

Example: | 0 | findings | <u>0</u> |

NOTES

> NOTES MADE FOLLOWING VISIT TO THE
> HUMPHREY DAVY MUSEUM OF MINING TECHNOLOGY
>
> Doors still closed at 10.12 a.m. – advertised hours 10 a.m. – 5 p.m. Man who unlocked
> door gave no reason, was rather rude and looked a mess. Cost £3 to get in – no ticket
> issued. Two exhibition rooms closed – no idea why. Two other rooms in semi-darkness.
> Six out of ten of the kinetic displays in the children's gallery did not work when the
> buttons were pressed. There were no labels on thirty exhibits and another ten had
> labels too close to the floor. The 'Ace Café' had run out of coffee and my 'Collier's
> sandwich' (prawn and mayonnaise) was probably left over from the day before.
> Conclusion – food AND actual visit very disappointing.

Dear Dr Crompton,

As part of our survey of local museums, a representative of the Barchester Consumers' Group visited your museum on 21st August. We are sure that, in the interests of providing a better service to the public, you would like to receive a summary of her **(0)** … .

It seems that although you advertise an **(62)** … of 10 a.m. there was a twelve-minute **(63)** … and **(64)** … was offered by the attendant who unlocked the door. In fact, his **(65)** … was rather unpleasant and his uniform could not be described **(66)** … . Our representative also reports that no ticket was issued in return for the **(67)** … of £3. Apparently, two exhibition rooms were closed without any explanation being given and two other rooms were inadequately **(68)** … . More than **(69)** … of the kinetic displays in the Children's Gallery were out **(70)** … . Labels were **(71)** … thirty exhibits and ten others had labels very close to the floor. Our representative was disappointed as coffee was **(72)** … and she reports that her sandwich was **(73)** … . In short, she felt that both **(74)** … and exhibition arrangements fell well below what the public has a right to expect.

If you have any comments to make on our observations, we will be delighted to discuss them with you.

Yours sincerely

Jane Smith

Part 6

For questions **75–80**, read the following text and then choose from the list **A–J** given below the best phrase to fill each of the spaces. Write one letter (**A–J**) in the correct box on your answer sheet. Each correct phrase may only be used once. **Some of the suggested answers do not fit at all.** The exercise begins with an example (**0**).

Example:

0	J	0

WORLD WAR I SHELLS

Twice a day throughout the summer in a field outside the small Belgian town of Poelkapelle, a strange ritual takes place. First, a siren sounds. Then a number of boxes are lowered into specially prepared pits. **(0)** ... , throwing clouds of earth into the air. **(75)** ... ; it is only another consignment of World War I shells exploding 75 years late.

Bomb disposal experts at Poelkapelle will be hard at work for many years to come. **(76)** ... , but best estimates suggest that of 1.5 billion shells fired on the Western Front between 1914 and 1918, about 30% failed to explode on impact. **(77)** ... , most of which are still out there. In the countryside around Poelkapelle, farmers plough up these deadly souvenirs almost daily. **(78)** ... ; after unearthing the shells they leave them by the roadside to be collected by an army jeep. The shells, however, remain potentially unstable and lethal as most of them are badly corroded after so many decades in the ground.

(79) ... . This is initially difficult because they are encrusted with rust and dirt. Officers used to clean them by hand in the open air. Now they use a high-pressure water jet or, if the dirt proves too stubborn, they remove it with a remote-control machine. **(80)** ... . Shells over 50 kilos have to be exploded at sea; the remainder are stored, ready to be detonated at the ritual hours of 11.45 am and 3.30 pm.

A   The local people are used to it

B   It does not say much for the quality control in the munitions factories of Britain and Germany

C   Only after positive identification of their country of origin can the shells be made safe

D   Most of the field guns used in World War I were very inaccurate at long range

E   Once cleaned and classified, the shells are placed in wooden boxes, separated by sand

F   That makes 400 million unexploded shells

G   These are dug out by army vehicles

H   Army personnel try to identify all types of shells

I   Over the years they have grown to treat them with a certain indifference

J   Shortly afterwards huge explosions rock the area

PAPER 4   LISTENING (approximately 45 minutes)

Part 1

You will hear a recording of a radio sports report. For questions **1–9**, complete the notes. You will need to write a number, a letter or a few words.

You will hear the recording **twice**.

Football results

1	England		South Korea	
2	Germany		Costa Rica	
3	Holland		USA	
4	Argentina		Austria	
5	Italy		Lithuania	

Boxing

Has a fight between Manuel Fernandez and Barry Jason definitely been arranged?   (Write yes/no)

	6

Golf

Who won last year's European title? **A** Philip Johnston
                                      B Bruce Chappell
                                      C Christian Bernhardt

	7

Why is Christian Bernhardt not playing in this year's competition?

	8

Tennis

How many times has Marina Stieff already won the Tournament?

	9

Part 2

You will hear the chairperson of the Technological Society making an announcement at the end of a meeting. For questions **10–19**, complete the information sheet. You will need to write a number or a few words.

Listen very carefully as you will hear the recording ONCE only.

The Technological Society

INTERNATIONAL DEPARTMENT

Course dates, fees and other expenses

Location: [_____ **10**] Brimston Square

Fee includes: [_____ **11**]

Extra costs: [_____ **12**]

[_____ **13**]

Overseas participants may incur extra costs

for: [_____ **14**]

Industrial Relations course	**Management Today course**
Cost: £ [**15**]	Cost: approx £ [**16**]
Length of courses: [**17**]	

Training Officers' course

Cost: £1,160 for Society members

£860 for [_____ **18**]

Length of course: [_____ **19**]

Part 3

You will hear part of a radio programme in which the interviewer is talking to a woman about a speech disorder known as 'stammering'. For questions **20–25**, choose the correct answer **A, B, C** or **D**.

You will hear the recording **twice**.

20 What does Anita Andrews feel about being on the radio?
   A   nervous
   B   proud
   C   grateful
   D   embarrassed

21 How was she treated at school?
   A   The teachers tended to be impatient.
   B   Her friends refused to play with her.
   C   The teachers asked her difficult questions.
   D   Her friends used to imitate her.

22 How did Joseph try to stop himself from stammering?
   A   by going to a speech therapist
   B   by avoiding his mother's speech patterns
   C   by speaking very quickly
   D   by talking as little as possible

23 Why did the speech unit insist on Joseph's parents attending the course?
   A   because stammering is a genetic defect
   B   because his mother was also a stammerer
   C   because Joseph found family life difficult
   D   because stammering can be related to family behaviour

24 What did Joseph's parents learn from the course?
   A   They had to believe that their son would improve.
   B   They had to face up to their son's stammer.
   C   They had to encourage Joseph to speak more slowly.
   D   They had to become more sensitive to the needs of others.

25 Why does Anita refer to the film 'A Fish Called Wanda'?
   A   because it shows how amusing a stammer can be
   B   because it shows how difficult it is to cure a stammer
   C   because it shows how destructive a stammer can be
   D   because it shows how a stammer can be inherited

Part 4

You will hear five short extracts in which different people give their views about various means of communication. Each extract has two questions. For questions **26–35**, choose the correct answer **A, B** or **C**.

You will hear the recording **twice**.

26 The **first speaker** feels that communicating by post is more
  A personal.
  B reliable.
  C impressive.

27 What does he feel about letters sent by fax?
  A They are less entertaining.
  B They are not worth keeping.
  C They are often badly written.

28 How does the **second speaker** feel about the phone?
  A dependent on it
  B irritated by it
  C resentful of it

29 Why doesn't she like answering machines?
  A Strange people leave messages.
  B Voices don't sound natural.
  C The machine makes odd noises.

30 What annoys the **third speaker** about mobile phones?
  A when they are used
  B how they are used
  C where they are used

31 When has he been disturbed by mobile phones?
  A when at home
  B when at work
  C when travelling

32 The **fourth speaker's** uncle
  A lived in a place without telephones.
  B had the telephone disconnected.
  C didn't see the need for a telephone.

33 How did the fourth speaker feel at receiving a telegram?
  A excited
  B guilty
  C embarrassed

34 Why does **speaker five** prefer the fax to the phone?
  A It allows her to work from home.
  B She gets a briefer response.
  C It doesn't interrupt her work.

35 Why does she find the fax annoying sometimes?
  A It makes too much noise.
  B It encourages people to be impatient.
  C Some of the messages are unclear.

PAPER 5   SPEAKING (15 minutes)

There are two examiners. One (the interlocutor) conducts the test, providing you with the necessary materials and explaining what you have to do. The other examiner (the assessor) will be introduced to you, but then takes no further part in the interaction.

Part 1 (3 minutes)
The interlocutor will first ask you and your partner a few questions. You will then be asked to find out some information about each other, on topics such as hobbies, interests, career plans, etc.

Part 2 (4 minutes)
You will each be given the opportunity to talk for about a minute, and to comment briefly after your partner has spoken.

   The interlocutor gives you a set of pictures and asks you to talk about them for about one minute. Each set of pictures has a different focus, so it is important to listen carefully to the interlocutor's instructions. The interlocutor then asks your partner a question about your pictures and your partner responds briefly.

   You will then be given another set of pictures to look at. Your partner talks about these pictures for about one minute. This time the interlocutor asks you a question about your partner's pictures and you respond briefly.

Part 3 (4 minutes)
In this part of the test you and your partner will be asked to talk together. The interlocutor will place a new set of pictures on the table between you. This stimulus provides the basis for a discussion. The interlocutor will explain what you have to do.

Part 4 (4 minutes)
The interlocutor will ask some further questions, which will lead to a more general discussion of what you have talked about in Part 3. You will be encouraged to comment on what your partner says, and the interlocutor will also take part in the discussion.

Test 3

PAPER 1   READING (1 hour 15 minutes)

Part 1

Answer questions **1–13** by referring to the newspaper article on page **57**.

For questions **1–13**, answer by choosing from the mountain regions (**A–H**). Some of the choices may be required more than once. Indicate your answers **on the separate answer sheet**.

Note: When more than one answer is required, these may be given **in any order**.

Harsh weather conditions can be found there.	**A** Bonnati Pillar
1 .... **2** **3**	**B** K2
Getting there is relatively cheap.	**C** The Andes
4	
No climb has been attempted there.	**D** Mount McKinley
5	**E** Tienshan
It takes a long time to get there.	
6	**F** Lhotse Middle
Climbers have to deal with bureaucracy there.	**G** The Eiger
7	
People have made solo climbs there.	**H** Everest
8 .... **9**	
Climbers come across man-made structures there.	
10	
Disasters continue to happen there.	
11	
It is not as easy to climb there as people say.	
12	
Only the best climbers make successful climbs there.	
13	

HIGH ADVENTURE

PLENTY of adventures are available to the climber who dares – on Everest alone, before you consider any other area of the world.

Given that ever since that historic moment at 11.30 am on May 29th 1953 when the Sherpa Tensing Norgay, GM, and Sir Edmund Hillary, KBE, became the first men to set foot on the world's highest peak, some 300 climbers have made it to the top of Everest by a variety of routes, one might be forgiven for supposing that that mountain held no more mystery and presented no more challenges. Especially when one remembers that in 1978 Rheinhold Messner and Peter Habeler did it without bottled oxygen, that in 1985 Messner became the first man to climb it alone, that Sherpa Sundare has climbed it five times, that the American Richard Bass reached the summit at the age of 55 years and 130 days, and that from 21st–30th April 1985, Arne Naess's Norwegian expedition succeeded in putting 17 people on the summit, including eight in one day.

Indeed, there is a feeling amongst mountaineers that, given sufficient resources, even the most inexperienced climber can look good on Everest. Permission is pretty easy to acquire provided one attends carefully enough to one's application and is sufficiently furnished with supplies of the hard folding stuff. (10,000 dollars should be enough to ensure an Everest booking for up to nine climbers.) And yet, no matter how many high altitude porters one may hire, or how state-of-the-art one's lightweight clothing and equipment, or how many fixed camps and ropes there may be in place on the way up, danger is always lurking around the next ridge: especially when the weather

turns. Late April to May is the best time to be in the Himalayas: before the monsoon hits.

Fortunately, there have not been any major catastrophes on Everest recently – which is more than can be said for K2. Though only two ropes' length short of Everest, this mountain could not be more different.

The Karakorams are set in the wildest imaginable landscape of range upon mountain range. Just to get one's first sight of K2 takes 12 days of hard walking from the nearest road, compared with the two days it takes from the Sherpa village of Namshe Bazaar to Everest Base Camp. And because bottled oxygen is hardly ever used on K2 (unlike Everest), it has the reputation (well-deserved) of being a real climber's mountain.

But however much the mountains of Asia may continue to seize the public imagination, for the climbers themselves there are plenty of other mountain ranges to be explored and more than enough challenges to be faced – in Russia, in South America, in Alaska, and in Europe.

The North Face of the Eiger, for example, is still considered a formidable adversary. Not only is one confronted with 9,000 feet of sheer climbing (most big Alpine faces are about 3,000 feet), but certain parts are very difficult to reverse climb in the event of bad weather. (There is an added surreal element in the shape of the doors set into the rock face which lead to the comfort and safety of the Jungfraujoch railways and which are often only inches away from the climbers' noses as they clamber past.)

There are always new routes to be negotiated at all levels of

climbing. Particularly in the Western Alps – Zermatt, the Mont Blanc Massif, the Bernese Oberland …

For those who wish to add an extra dimension of discomfort to their hardship, Mount McKinley in Alaska enjoys the distinction of being the coldest mountain in the world. The Andean peaks of Peru, Ecuador and Bolivia are blessed with some of the most reliable weather to be found anywhere, and are set amidst some of the most enchanting bird, plant and animal life imaginable. As for Russia, an increasing number of climbers are heading for the Caucasus, for the Pamirs, where there are three 7,000-metre peaks still to be climbed, and for Tienshan, where there are a further two.

Not least of the joys of climbing in Russia is the ease and lack of serious expense (100 dollars a day) with which the international Mountain Camps lay on helicopter flights to the base camps. You wouldn't get two minutes in the Alps for that!

These days, solo climbing seems to be all the rage. Everyone got very excited last summer when Catherine Destevel made a solo ascent of the Bonnati Pillar despite the fact that Bonnati himself was alone when he first did it. But in British mountaineering circles at least, such feats are not held to be important. Not when there are still summits to be climbed, like Lhotse Middle – a fearsome ridge, 8,500 metres up on the Everest massif between Lhotse and Nuptse, so tortuous and so inaccessible that no one has yet pitted their skills against it. But they will. Everything will be climbed one day.

Part 2

For questions **14–20**, choose which of the paragraphs **A–H** on page **59** fit into the numbered gaps in the magazine article below. There is one extra paragraph, which does not fit in any of the gaps.

Indicate your answers **on the separate answer sheet**.

BRINGING UP BADGERS

'What now?' was my immediate thought, as one of my helpers carried a cardboard box towards me. Since my husband Derek and I turned our dairy farm in Somerset into an 'open farm' six years ago, we've established a reputation for looking after orphaned animals. But the noise coming from the box – a cross between a cackle and a bark – was not one I recognised, so it was with great interest that I peered in to see three small grey badger cubs, each no more than eight inches long. Their coats (later to reveal fleas) were like velvet, and milky-coloured eyes looked up at me from three tiny black-and-white striped heads.

14

I could see they were healthy and well but they were cold and whimpering. After defleaing them, I took them into the farmhouse kitchen and installed them beside the stove for warmth. There were two females, Primrose and Bluebell, and a male, Willow. Initially I used a syringe to feed them but each cub had to be wiped with a warm cloth first to simulate the sensation of the mother licking them. This encouraged them to empty their bowels and bladder. For the first two or three days they were fed every four hours.

15

The vet's post mortem revealed that Willow had died from a lung infection. When bottle feeding any animal it is important not to let it drink too fast, as liquid can overflow into the lungs. In Willow's case this had caused an infection that would have been difficult to rectify, even with the help of antibiotics, in one so small.

16

Willow II joined the fold. At six weeks, he was about two weeks younger than the females and over the next few days I discovered why his mother had left him. Never had anything been so difficult to feed. To place the bottle's teat in his mouth and cajole him into drinking I had to keep moving it around and squeezing it. After a full 10 minutes he would latch on to it as if he had not drunk all day. By the end of April the females were weaned on to creamed rice and then literally anything. It was to be a different story for Willow. He was happy to give up the bottle but could not master the habit of eating without walking through his food, tipping it over or just sitting

in it. Eventually I offered him a sausage, which little by little was chewed, played with and finally eaten. After a week of sausages he was ready to move on to something else.

17

By August my foundlings had begun to turn nocturnal and would go for walks only at dusk or late at night. We often went through the cider orchard; in its long grass, everyone was fair game. The cubs would get excited, ruffle up their fur so that they looked like snowballs and chase each other's tails. As 'human badgers' we were included in this sport. I learnt to avoid those playful charges that ended with a sharp nip, but Derek accompanied us only occasionally and so never grasped this skill: his reactions to being 'caught' were sometimes as colourful as his bruises.

18

The local press took some pictures of me walking the badgers, and such was the response that we started an appeal to build a sett on the farm for the badgers to move into. With advice freely given, we designed our badgers' new home. Daniel, one of our sons, drew up the plans and we built a sett complete with tunnels, an enclosure and a badger gate facing the same way as their nightly walks.

19	

The cost of the building work was far more than we envisaged but a local bus company (the aptly named Badgerline) sponsored part of the appeal, and local firms donated building materials. Every-one, it seemed, wanted to see the badgers with a home of their own.

20	

These days my walks with them are not as regular, especially as they are not fully awake until midnight. We see Primrose only occasionally (she has joined a neighbouring sett) but Bluebell and Willow II still rush up to say hello before they go dashing off into the night. This is their territory now, an area that they have come to know well and a home they have readily accepted.

A At nearly five months old, they were all eating cereals for breakfast; a meat and vegetable meal for lunch and fruit and nuts, cheese, hard boiled eggs and sunflower seeds in the evening. The usual diet for badgers is 60 per cent earthworms, plus beetles and bugs, baby rabbits, mice and voles and even shoots or roots of plants. Certainly my badgers were much better off than other cubs that year; the summer was exceptionally hot and digging for earthworms must have been almost impossible.

B Disheartened by my failure, I continued rearing the others. But fate works in strange ways: six days later a local farmer, who had heard about our cubs, came to see me. Behind some silage bags he had discovered a single male cub, abandoned by its mother. He knew she would not return; the area had been disturbed too much and already the cub was cold and hungry.

C I had never seen badger cubs before. As most of them are born between mid-January and mid-March, they usually spend their early life underground and, if orphaned, die of starvation, never to be found. These three had been brought in by building contractors; while laying drain pipes, their machinery had bored into the sett before they realised it. The mother was found dead with her babies still suckling her.

D This didn't happen with the females, but poor Willow was true to form. Before long, apart from his definite striped head, we had a totally bald badger. He was healthy, but because badgers tug on each other's skin in play, games proved rather painful.

E Within a week the cubs had progressed to drinking from a bottle and were moving around, albeit shakily. With each other for company and a heated pad as a substitute 'mum', they seemed very contented. Three weeks after their arrival, however, I noticed that Willow seemed lethargic, although he was still taking food as normal. It was a warning sign. I should have reacted straightaway; not realising its importance, I awoke the next morning to find him dead.

F It had three chambers, one slightly larger than the others, with a glass side to enable people to see into the sett from a darkened enclosure. As the sett began to take shape, the badgers would explore it before going on their walks. Eventually walks were forgotten in the excitement of climbing through the tunnels and sorting out bedding.

G Early one evening they finally moved in. After watching them for a while, we left them to settle. Half an hour later I crept back to see if all was well, to be met with the sight of three badgers curled up in their chambers sound asleep.

H It was during two of these late-night walks in the very dry period that I spotted other badgers in our field. Presumably they were having to extend their territories to find enough food, although badgers are very territorial and will kill others that wander into their territory. We were even warned that they would climb into our badger pen and kill the cubs, so sheet metal was placed over the gate to make it as inaccessible as possible.

Part 3

Read the following article from a magazine and answer questions **21–25** on page **61**. On your answer sheet, indicate the letter **A**, **B**, **C** or **D** against the number of each question. Give only one answer to each question.

Indicate your answers **on the separate answer sheet**.

Blacksmiths

THROUGHOUT the ages, iron has exerted a powerful pull on the human imagination, and the men who work it have often been regarded as much more than skilled craftsmen. Before the Industrial Revolution, blacksmiths enjoyed the same status as doctors and astrologers, because they were the sole providers of weapons, armour and farming tools.

They have also been fêted as artists. Eighteenth-century smiths produced the wonderfully baroque ironwork for St Paul's Cathedral. The sinuous metal-work of French and Belgian Art Nouveau architecture was always the work of a talented blacksmith.

But practitioners of these ancient skills had become almost extinct in Britain by the late 1960s, for heavy industry had ceased to have any use for them, and tower-block architects rarely used any-thing as graceful and pleasing as a wrought-iron handrail.

Over the past 10 years, however, there has been something of a revival – thanks to greater interest in decorative architecture and a less conservative approach to interior design. Even so, much of the work looks surprisingly clichéd: manu-facturers of gates and balconies still advertise their wares as 'classical' or 'Victorian-style'. You can't walk into a trendy design store without

being assailed by rusty candlesticks with dangly bits.

Thankfully, alternatives exist and a series of events over the next few weeks aims to promote the blacksmith's craft. The first of these, an exhibition of forged iron-work by members of the British Artist Blacksmiths Association (BABA), opened last week at the Fire & Iron gallery in Leatherhead, Surrey.

Alan Dawson, the secretary of BABA, says: 'We could be at the start of a new Iron Age, because, in a sense, both the general public and blacksmiths have had their blinkers removed.' Power tools have liberated smiths from all that labouring over a hot anvil, and they can now bend, split, twist and spot-weld the metal with relative ease. 'In short,' says Dawson, 'these artists now have a material which allows them to express themselves.'

About 250 pieces have been produced for the show, ranging from bookends to a spiral stair-case. Reserve prices start at £90 and climb well into four figures. Most of the money raised will go to individual makers, 'but a per-centage of every sale will be retained by the Association for the promotion of good ironwork,' says Dawson.

His own contributions consist

of an eight-foot gate, and a stan-dard lamp topped with a mouth-blown glass shade.

'My style results from just allowing steel to bend and flow into shape when it's hot. It's a bit like drawing with metal in space,' he says.

Many of the artists admit to being fascinated by iron. Unlike most metals, which are relatively malleable when cold, iron and steel are a tougher, more demanding medium. Susan May, a jeweller by training, says, 'It's quite magical, because it's incredibly soft when it's hot, but as soon as it cools down, it becomes really rigid and immovable again.'

Ann Catrin Evans' mild steel door-knockers and handles seem to have been inspired by those bleak castles that are a stock fea-ture of horror films. One of her designs is shaped like a ball and chain, another like a Celtic cross. 'I love the fact that steel is cold and hard,' she says. 'And the way it feels as though it's there forever.'

No other base metal can have given man as much visual pleasure, or a greater feeling of security. The chances of iron being used deco-ratively for the next thousand years are good, to say the least – as long as we don't have to look at any more rusty candlesticks, that is.

21 Interest in blacksmiths' work has revived because
   A   they have developed a number of new skills.
   B   people have started to want variety in design.
   C   gates and balconies have come back into fashion.
   D   they now produce better-quality products.

22 What is the aim of the BABA exhibition?
   A   To demonstrate the modern blacksmith at work.
   B   To encourage people to become blacksmiths.
   C   To promote the tools available to blacksmiths.
   D   To show what modern blacksmiths can produce.

23 Some of the profits from the show will be used
   A   to start an association of blacksmiths.
   B   to purchase good materials for blacksmiths to use.
   C   to publicise high-quality goods made by blacksmiths.
   D   to run training courses for blacksmiths.

24 Susan May likes using iron because
   A   it is perfect for making jewellery.
   B   it can easily be shaped when cold.
   C   it is challenging to work with.
   D   it becomes cool very quickly.

25 Which of the following statements best expresses the writer's view?
   A   The art of decorative ironwork is likely to survive.
   B   The revival of interest in blacksmiths will be short-lived.
   C   Old-fashioned ironwork will come back into fashion.
   D   Blacksmiths are unfortunately a thing of the past.

Part 4

Answer questions **26–41** by referring to the newspaper article on pages **63** and **64**.

For questions **26–32**, answer by choosing from the goods (**A–H**). Some of the choices may be required more than once. Indicate your answers **on the separate answer sheet**.

Note: When more than one answer is required, these may be given **in any order**.

placing goods next to items they go together with	**A** washing powders
26	**B** tea
dispersing goods around the store	**C** vegetables
27 .... **28**	**D** salad dressing
displaying the goods in small quantities only	**E** dairy products
29	**F** bread
having the goods appropriately lit	
30 .... **31**	**G** ready-made meals
making sure these goods are the first things people see	**H** clothes
32	

For questions **33–41**, answer by choosing from the sections of the article (**A–I**). Some choices may be required more than once.

Note: When more than one answer is required, these may be given **in any order**.

crime prevention	**33**		
interior decoration	**34**	**35**	**36** ....
customers who always buy the same brands	**37**		
goods that are not profit-making	**38**		
customers' movements around the store	**39**	**40**	**41** ....

TALKING SHOP

Ever entered a store and come away with more than you intended to buy? We reveal the selling devices shops use that are designed to make you spend, spend, spend.

A The image of freshness

Supermarkets know from their market research that shoppers place a premium on fresh produce being in stores. They may place their fruit and veg at the entrance of a store, or even a display of house plants for sale, to enhance this. They may also provide an in-store bakery that wafts irresistible fresh bread smells around a large area of the store. The colour of the store's fixtures may heighten the image, too – for example, green may be used because of its association with fresh produce. The bulk of what supermarkets sell – pre-packaged grocery items such as frozen foods and washing powders – may be quite different from this image.

B Displaying to advantage

The location of products in the store is considered all-important in determining how well a particular brand sells. Nowhere is this more developed than in supermarkets. With computerised stock-control, supermarkets can find out the parts of the store from which shoppers will select items most often. In these areas can be found products with the highest mark-ups or ones which, though less profitable, sell very quickly. Traditionally in retailing, 'eye-level' means 'buy-level' – shelves at eye height are eagerly sought by manufacturers, or may be reserved for certain own-brand items. 'Dump bins' containing special offers tempt those who find it hard to resist a bargain. Increasingly popular is 'complementation' – placing dessert or salad dressings, say, over units containing ice-creams or items that may be eaten with salads such as burgers.

C Spreading staples around the store

Supermarkets may spread low price staples such as bread, tea and sugar around their stores and a long way from the entrance – shoppers have to pass tempting, higher-profit lines on the way. In similar vein, chainstores may locate the products they have a good reputation for as far away from the store entrance as possible. They can rely on a degree of customer loyalty towards these products, so they gamble that shoppers will go actively looking for them around the store, passing other wares that might tempt them.

D Less sells more

Chainstores have transformed the presentation of their wares in recent years. Much of the pioneering work has been done by the *Next* chain, which turned away from the 'pile them high, sell them cheap' approach to popular fashion. *Next* stores have a 'boutique' appeal – they're noted for displaying limited fashion-wear on the shelves, giving the impression that the merchandise is exclusive. Of course, *Next*'s clothing is not less mass-produced than that of their rivals – the company's success is as much a testament to good store design as it is to well-designed clothing.

E Tempting totals

Food shoppers, it seems, are more responsive to the overall size of their weekly or fortnightly bill than to the prices of individual items. Supermarkets take advantage of this by stocking a mix of low mark-up staples and high mark-up items, so it shouldn't be assumed everything that a supermarket sells is cheap. Low prices are of direct appeal to the thrifty shopper.

It's often said that supermarkets deliberately lose money on certain staples to draw shoppers in – known as 'loss leaders'. More commonly, their low prices are achieved by buying in huge quantities from manufacturers, by offering them a prominent place to display their products or by exceeding sales targets – all of which attract big discounts from the manufacturers.

F The all-important price-tag

Shoppers tend to buy fewer items in chainstores and may be more aware of individual pricing as a result. So the importance of pricing, say, a blouse at £14.99 as opposed to £15, still holds. (It's also a useful device, apparently, to reduce theft among the shop's own staff, who are obliged to ring up a sale in order to give the penny change.)

G Lighting to effect

Both supermarkets and chainstores give careful thought to lighting. With chainstores, the aim is to achieve lighting which is as close to natural light as possible so that shoppers get a fair idea of what the colour of the clothes will be like in daylight. With supermarkets, special lighting (and mirrors) may be used to enhance certain foods, particularly fresh fruit and veg.

H Walk this way

Many chainstores have divided up their floors with different carpeting – one pattern for the routes through a store and one defining sales areas. Shoppers are drawn naturally along these routes – known within the trade as the 'Yellow Brick Road'. It's not always successful – some shoppers are reluctant to stray off the routes into the sales areas. *Marks and Spencer*, for example, use wood or marble covering for routes, encouraging shoppers to walk on to the more welcoming carpet in sales areas.

I In-store promotion

As you enter a supermarket, giant colour photographs of succulent roasts, fancy cakes and cheeses hit you – irresistible if you've had nothing to eat before setting out on your shopping trip. In the United States, 'video trolleys' are being tried out in a number of supermarkets. Each trolley has a screen which advertises products as you shop. Sensors at the end of shelves trigger relevant advertising – so the shopper passing the cook-chill cabinets, say, may receive an ad. on the screen for ready-made moussaka. Such trolleys are aimed unashamedly at the impulse shopper, and the makers claim they increase sales by around 30 per cent.

PAPER 2   WRITING (2 hours)

Part 1

You **must** answer this question.

1   Last month you spent a week in England for High Life Travel as an interpreter for a group of tourists from your country. Unfortunately you and many members of the group were unhappy with the programme. High Life Travel has invited you to take part again as an interpreter but you feel that the conditions should be improved.

Read the advertisement for the holiday, an extract from a recent letter from a friend and, on page **66**, the programme with your notes based on the week when you were working.

Then, **using the information carefully**, write a **letter** to High Life Travel **accepting** the job but **suggesting** how the week's programme and your conditions of employment should be improved.

Holiday of your Dreams

⋆ a week in England in a luxury hotel ⋆
⋆ famous London sights ⋆
⋆ excursions out of London ⋆
⋆ excellent value ⋆

For more information, contact:

High Life Travel
4 Seed Street
London SW1Y 4BZ
Tel: 0207 384 1727

I can't believe what you told me about your job – to think that more than half the people were ready to go home by the third day! It hardly seems fair considering what it cost. Also, paying you so little (although, as you say, you weren't a professional interpreter) AND then not paying your expenses – I'd think twice about working for them again!

'High Life' programme

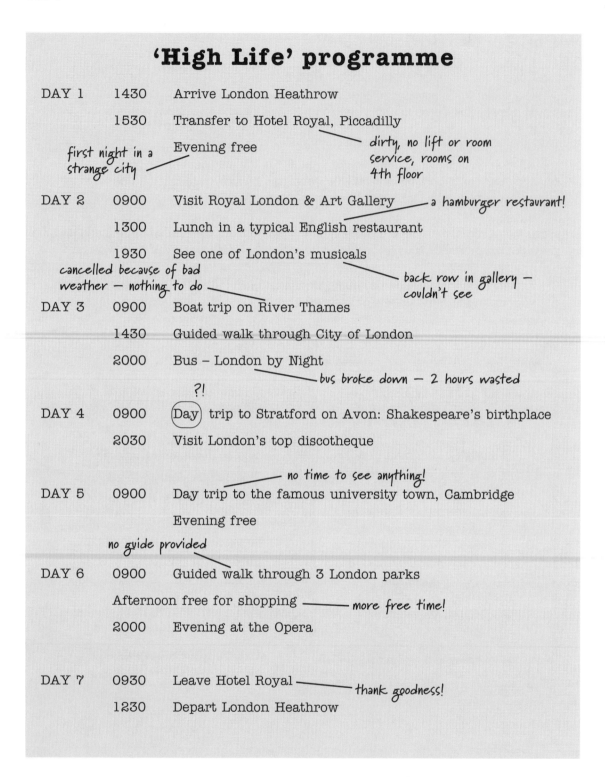

DAY 1   1430   Arrive London Heathrow

        1530   Transfer to Hotel Royal, Piccadilly

first night in a strange city   Evening free — *dirty, no lift or room service, rooms on 4th floor*

DAY 2   0900   Visit Royal London & Art Gallery — *a hamburger restaurant!*

        1300   Lunch in a typical English restaurant

        1930   See one of London's musicals

cancelled because of bad weather — nothing to do   *back row in gallery — couldn't see*

DAY 3   0900   Boat trip on River Thames

        1430   Guided walk through City of London

        2000   Bus – London by Night

?!   — *bus broke down — 2 hours wasted*

DAY 4   0900   (Day) trip to Stratford on Avon: Shakespeare's birthplace

        2030   Visit London's top discotheque

— no time to see anything!

DAY 5   0900   Day trip to the famous university town, Cambridge

        Evening free

no guide provided

DAY 6   0900   Guided walk through 3 London parks

        Afternoon free for shopping — *more free time!*

        2000   Evening at the Opera

DAY 7   0930   Leave Hotel Royal — *thank goodness!*

        1230   Depart London Heathrow

Now write the **letter** to High Life Travel (about 250 words). You do not need to include postal addresses.

Part 2

Choose **one** of the following writing tasks. Your answer should follow exactly the instructions given. Write approximately 250 words.

2

Do you use English at college or at work? The *English-users Newsletter* would like to hear from you about any problems you have experienced when using English and any benefits you have gained. We're sure you've got some interesting things to say to people in situations similar to yours, and we're keen to publish articles with as many different viewpoints as possible.

Write an **article** for the newsletter and share your views with people in a similar situation.

3   In a London museum there is to be an exhibition of some items of great interest from your country, and you have been asked to assist with the publicity. Write a **leaflet** which outlines the history of the items and explains their importance within and outside your country.

Write your **leaflet**.

4   An international English language magazine is preparing an article comparing attitudes to the changing role of women in different parts of the world at the end of the twentieth century, and you have been asked to write about the subject with specific reference to the situation in your own country. Write your **contribution to the article**, focusing on one or more of the following areas: the workplace and careers; marriage and relationships; housework; politics; education.

Write your **contribution**.

5   Someone in your community whom you have known for a long time wants to spend a year looking after children in an English-speaking family, and has asked you to write a character reference. You should write a detailed **reference**, indicating how long and in what capacity you have known this person, the strengths and weaknesses of their personality, and why you would support their application.

Write your **reference**.

PAPER 3   ENGLISH IN USE (1 hour 30 minutes)

Part 1

For questions **1–15**, read the text below and then decide which word on page **69** best fits each space. Put the letter you choose for each question in the correct box on your answer sheet. The exercise begins with an example **(0)**.

Example: | 0 | B | | 0 |

BECOMING A TRANSLATOR

The role of the translator in enabling literature to pass beyond its natural frontiers is receiving growing recognition. In **(0)** ... of the general increase in this **(1)** ... , it is not surprising that many people with literary interests and a knowledge of languages should think of adopting translating as a full- or part-time **(2)** ... . Some advice may usefully be **(3)** ... to such would-be translators.

The first difficulty the beginner will **(4)** ... is the unwillingness of publishers to entrust a translation to anyone who has not already **(5)** ... a reputation for sound work. The least publishers will **(6)** ... before commissioning a translation is a fairly lengthy **(7)** ... of the applicant's work, even if unpublished. Perhaps the best way the would-be translator can begin is to select some book of the type which he or she feels competent and **(8)** ... to translate, translate a **(9)** ... section of the book and then submit the book and the translation to a **(10)** ... publisher. If he or she is extremely lucky, this may **(11)** ... in a commission to translate the book. More **(12)** ... , however, publishers will **(13)** ... the book as such but if they are favourably **(14)** ... by the translation, they may very possibly commission some other book of a **(15)** ... nature which they already have in mind.

0   **A**   regard   **B**   view   **C**   awareness   **D**   consideration

1   **A**   field   **B**   category   **C**   ground   **D**   class

2   **A**   work   **B**   employment   **C**   occupation   **D**   line

3   **A**   made   **B**   given   **C**   told   **D**   shown

4   **A**   encounter   **B**   involve   **C**   reveal   **D**   introduce

5   **A**   formed   **B**   set   **C**   founded   **D**   established

6   **A**   instruct   **B**   oblige   **C**   demand   **D**   direct

7   **A**   instance   **B**   case   **C**   specimen   **D**   model

8   **A**   eager   **B**   nervous   **C**   agitated   **D**   excited

9   **A**   substantial   **B**   main   **C**   grand   **D**   plentiful

10 **A**   fit   **B**   right   **C**   convenient   **D**   suitable

11 **A**   finish   **B**   lead   **C**   effect   **D**   result

12 **A**   surely   **B**   probably   **C**   certainly   **D**   expectedly

13 **A**   exclude   **B**   reject   **C**   object   **D**   disapprove

14 **A**   impressed   **B**   convinced   **C**   affected   **D**   taken

15 **A**   common   **B**   same   **C**   similar   **D**   joint

Part 2

For questions **16–30**, complete the following article by writing each missing word in the correct box on your answer sheet. **Use only one word for each space**. The exercise begins with an example **(0)**.

Example: | 0 | do | | 0 |

A START IN SAILING

Ask any sports enthusiast to name the most popular sports and the stock answer will probably be football, cricket, golf and rugby. A lot of people **(0)** ... play those games but far **(16)** ... go fishing, play badminton or sail. Why do we get it wrong? Because sports editors, of newspapers and television channels, are stuck **(17)** ... their traditional patterns of judging by crowds **(18)** ... than by how many actually go out and do the thing. Sailing probably suffers most **(19)** ... this narrow-mindedness **(20)** ... it is often difficult to report and almost impossible to film except **(21)** ... huge expense.

Yet, despite the absence of the oxygen of publicity, sailing is **(22)** ... of the most popular participant sports. Why is it so popular in Britain? Possibly because of the great island tradition of **(23)** ... a nation of sailors, but probably much more because of **(24)** ... many opportunities. Nowhere in Britain is all that far from the sea and **(25)** ... are plenty of rivers and lakes where it is easy to get afloat. But many would-be sailors are discouraged **(26)** ... taking the first steps. They worry **(27)** ... the cost of a boat, the need for special equipment, the dangers of tackling the elemental forces of nature and believe that sailing-club people **(28)** ... snobbish and unapproachable. All misconceptions. You can start sailing **(29)** ... next to nothing and find friendly sailing clubs throughout the country **(30)** ... nobody is snobbish or looks down on beginners.

Part 3

In **most** lines of the following text, there is **either** a spelling **or** a punctuation error. For each numbered line **31–46**, write the correctly spelled word or show the correct punctuation in the box on your answer sheet. **Some lines are correct.** Indicate these lines with a tick (✔) in the box. The exercise begins with three examples **(0)**, **(00)** and **(000)**.

Examples:

0	think that	0
00	definitely	0
000	✔	0

COSTUME JEWELLERY

0   It may seem a little ridiculous to think, that people deliberately buy

00   anything artificial but that is most definately true of costume jewellery

000 from the 1930s, which now sells for vast sums of money and is

31   increasingly popular in America Europe and Asia. The term 'costume

32   jewellery' is relatively new but such jewellery has been around ever since

33   people first started to decorrate themselves with bones and shells. The

34   Romans, in particular took delight in making fake jewels from glass and

35   ceramics and combining them with preciuos stones and metal. The

36   eighteenth century saw an improvment with the arrival of hand-cut glass,

37   now referred to as paste'. This became so fashionable and sought after

38   that it rivalled diamons in both demand and price. Good pieces of

39   genuinely antique paste jewellery still sell for hundreds and sometimes

40   even thousands' of pounds. The real revolution in costume jewellery is

41   attributed to the french designer Coco Chanel, who turned it away from pure

42   immitation of previous designs in favour of 'jewels' made to be valued

43   in their own right. Plastics were used, to produce shapes and colours

44   never seen before, let alone worn, and they completly revolutionised the

45   jewellery market. These plastic creations rapidly gained popularity and

46   became easily affordible, which naturally meant that fashions in jewellery

     changed ever more quickly.

Part 4

For questions **47–61**, read the two texts on pages **72** and **73**. Use the words in the boxes to the right of the texts to form **one** word that fits in the same numbered space in the text. Write the new word in the correct box on your answer sheet. The exercise begins with an example **(0)**.

Example: | 0 | frequently | 0 |

MAGAZINE ARTICLE

KNOW YOUR ONIONS

We **(0)** ... take onions for granted, but there are so many different, delicious **(47)** ... that Peter Smith claims it's **(48)** ... to imagine cooking without them.

In the USA they boast that onions are so sweet they can be eaten like apples. Well, I'm not quite that **(49)** ... but I do love onion soup, onion tart, and whole, roasted onions served with herb butter. I have a particular **(50)** ... for red onions; their colour and flavour makes eating them in salads absolute **(51)** ... .

Spring onions have the mildest of flavours – they're delicious **(52)** ... grilled on the barbecue, and taste wonderful with fish. Finally, the small onions called shallots are **(53)** ... for more delicate sauces. As you can see, a cook can't live without onions.

(0)	FREQUENT
(47)	VARY
(48)	POSSIBLE
(49)	ENTHUSIASM
(50)	PREFER
(51)	PERFECT
(52)	BRIEF
(53)	ESSENCE

HOLIDAY ADVERTISEMENT

HOLIDAY OF A LIFETIME

A Dreamcamp holiday is an **(54)** … experience shaped only by your own choices.

It's spontaneous – you can do as much or as little as you like. And you can go where you want, when you want.

It's really **(55)** … . Dreamcamp offers a wide range of **(56)** … in locations all over the world. With a different **(57)** … on each site, there's so much to do. But if your energy isn't as **(58)** … as the activities on offer, you can just relax!

It's extremely **(59)** … – our tents have plenty of room, well equipped kitchens, proper beds, and lots more!

Let the kids have fun! We'll take care of the children so you can take it easy. All in all it's a fantastic, **(60)** … , family holiday, **(61)** … as the kids go free!

(54)	ORDINARY
(55)	ADVENTURE
(56)	ACTIVE
(57)	SELECT
(58)	END
(59)	SPACE
(60)	AFFORD
(61)	SPECIAL

Part 5

For questions **62–74**, read the following informal note and use the information in it to complete the numbered gaps in the more formal letter. The words you need **do not occur** in the informal note. **Use no more than two words for each gap**. The exercise begins with an example **(0)**.

Example:

0	As requested	0

INFORMAL NOTE

I've been asked to write a reference for Faith Good. Do you think you could help me with it? It's quite hard to know how to write a diplomatic reference for her as she isn't exactly the ideal employee. Mind you, she means well and I'd like to help her get a good job. She passed her typing and shorthand course after all and I think she's good at speaking to people over the phone. She's not bad at Spanish and she has her own car – passed her driving test last month, I believe. She's a fitness fanatic and she always wears the latest fashions. She's always cracking jokes – even if some of them are pretty terrible – and she certainly doesn't worry in the slightest about talking to new people. So she fits the bill as far as the job is concerned in quite a few ways. I guess I can't avoid mentioning her appalling spelling and the way she's late for everything. I suppose I could finish by saying – and I think this is true really – that we'd be sorry to see her go if another company gave her a job somewhere else. And I could add that we'd be happy to give any other details they want about what she actually does here at the moment.

FORMAL LETTER

Dear Mr Brown,

   (0) ... I am sending you a reference for Ms Faith Good. I am happy to recommend her for the position you have advertised. She has a **(62)** ... typing and shorthand and she has a good telephone **(63)** ... . She speaks Spanish **(64)** ... and she holds a **(65)** ... . Faith is **(66)** ... aerobics and running and she always dresses **(67)** ... . She has a **(68)** ... of humour and is **(69)** ... about meeting new people. She is certainly, therefore, in many ways **(70)** ... the job that you are advertising. Although her spelling could **(71)** ... and she tends not to be **(72)** ... , we would genuinely miss her many qualities if she were to accept **(73)** ... of employment elsewhere. Please do not hesitate to contact me if you require any further information about Ms Good's **(74)** ... .

   Yours sincerely,

   Jenny Smith

Part 6

For questions **75–80**, read the following text and then choose from the list **A–J** given below the best sentence to fill each of the spaces. Write one letter (**A–J**) in the correct box on your answer sheet. Each correct sentence may only be used once. **Some of the suggested answers do not fit at all.** The exercise begins with an example **(0)**.

Example: | **0** | **J** | | **0** |

CHILDREN AND FAILURE

My seventeen-month-old niece caught sight of my ballpoint pen the other day and reached out for it. It has a plastic cap that fits over the point. **(0)** … . After looking it over, she put it back on. Then off again; then on again. **(75)** … . Now if I want to be able to use my pen, I have to keep it out of sight, for when she sees it, she wants to play with it. She is so deft at putting it back on that it makes me wonder about all I've read about lack of coordination in infants. **(76)** … . These quiet summer days I spend many hours watching this baby. What comes across most vividly is that she is a kind of scientist. **(77)** … . Most of her waking time she is intensely and purposefully active, soaking up experience and trying to make sense of it, trying to find how things around her behave and trying to make them behave as she wants them to.

In the face of what looks like unbroken failure she is so persistent. **(78)** … . But she goes right on, not the least daunted. **(79)** … . Even a five-year-old is often embarrassed by mistakes, let alone an adult, but she is not. **(80)** … .

A Perhaps this is because she has not yet learnt to feel ashamed of defeat
B It is a difficult job, even for an adult
C Unlike her elders, she is not concerned with protecting herself
D She is always observing and experimenting
E It was a great surprise to everyone
F A good game
G Most of her experiments don't work
H They may be much more skilful than we think
I There is nothing she will not meddle with

J She took hold of it, and after some pushing and pulling, got the cap off

PAPER 4 LISTENING (approximately 45 minutes)

Part 1

You will hear a recording of an interview with Edward Munns, a representative from the Lighting Industry Federation. He is talking about a new type of environmentally-friendly lightbulb.
For questions **1–8**, complete the information.

You will hear the recording **twice**.

Comparison of standard lightbulb with new type:				
	Ordinary standard bulb		Environmentally-friendly bulb	
Expected life in number of hours		**1**		
Expected life in years if used 3 hours/day		**2**		**3**
Average cost				**4**
Current sales in UK		**5**		**6**
Probable supplier				**7**
Possible saving on electricity costs				**8**

Part 2

Look at the plan of Bankeira, an archaeological site. You will hear a tour guide conducting a party of visitors around the site. For questions **9–18**, fill in the name of each building in the appropriate space.

Listen very carefully as you will hear the recording ONCE only.

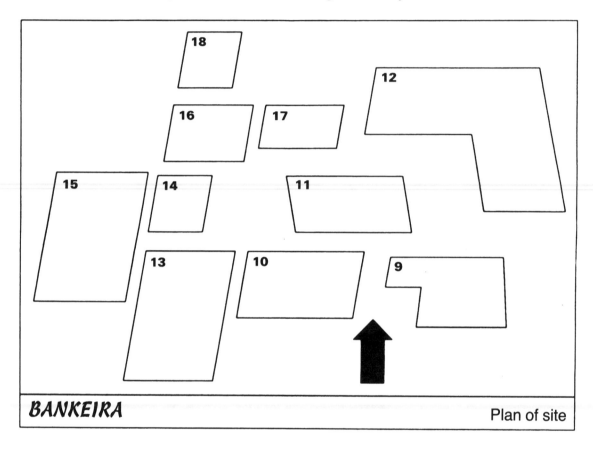

BANKEIRA

Plan of site

Part 3

You will hear part of a radio interview with the actress Susan Davenant who is starring in a successful TV series called 'The Falling Leaves'. For questions **19–23**, choose the correct answer from **A, B, C** or **D**.

You will hear the recording **twice**.

19 Why did Susan enjoy making the series?
   A   It was a success.
   B   Everything went right.
   C   She knew everybody.
   D   Everyone got on well.

20 What made Susan walk off the set?
   A   She disliked repeating the scene.
   B   Her colleagues were angry with her.
   C   The director criticised her acting.
   D   She lost patience with herself.

21 Why did she make an effort to put on weight?
   A   She was afraid of losing the part.
   B   Some special costumes did not fit her.
   C   She felt it would help her play the part.
   D   She did not like her appearance.

22 How does she feel about being recognised by fans?
   A   She feels rather annoyed.
   B   She still finds it embarrassing.
   C   She feels it is an invasion of privacy.
   D   She accepts it as part of being well-known.

23 What is Susan's ambition?
   A   To become famous for her work in theatre.
   B   To direct a classical stage play.
   C   To act in as many films as possible.
   D   To develop her part in 'The Falling Leaves'.

Part 4

You will hear five short extracts, in which various people are talking about food.

TASK ONE

For questions **24–28**, match the extracts as you hear them with the people listed **A–H**.

TASK TWO

For questions **29–33**, match the extracts as you hear them with each speaker's intention, listed **A–H**.

A	Dietary expert		24
B	Food manufacturer		25
C	Chef		26
D	Customer in restaurant		27
E	Parent		28
F	Neighbour		
G	Restaurant critic		
H	Guest at dinner		

A	giving advice on cooking		29
B	warning		30
C	criticising		31
D	recommending types of food		32
E	praising		33
F	trying to persuade		
G	expressing disgust		
H	giving advice on slimming		

Remember that you must complete both tasks as you listen. You will hear the recording twice.

PAPER 5   SPEAKING (15 minutes)

There are two examiners. One (the interlocutor) conducts the test, providing you with the necessary materials and explaining what you have to do. The other examiner (the assessor) will be introduced to you, but then takes no further part in the interaction.

Part 1 (3 minutes)
The interlocutor will first ask you and your partner a few questions. You will then be asked to find out some information about each other, on topics such as hobbies, interests, career plans, etc.

Part 2 (4 minutes)
You will each be given the opportunity to talk for about a minute, and to comment briefly after your partner has spoken.

   The interlocutor gives you a set of pictures and asks you to talk about them for about one minute. Each set of pictures has a different focus, so it is important to listen carefully to the interlocutor's instructions. The interlocutor then asks your partner a question about your pictures and your partner responds briefly.

   You will then be given another set of pictures to look at. Your partner talks about these pictures for about one minute. This time the interlocutor asks you a question about your partner's pictures and you respond briefly.

Part 3 (4 minutes)
In this part of the test you and your partner will be asked to talk together. The interlocutor will place a new set of pictures on the table between you. This stimulus provides the basis for a discussion. The interlocutor will explain what you have to do.

Part 4 (4 minutes)
The interlocutor will ask some further questions, which will lead to a more general discussion of what you have talked about in Part 3. You will be encouraged to comment on what your partner says, and the interlocutor will also take part in the discussion.

Test 4

PAPER 1 READING (1 hour 15 minutes)

Part 1

Answer questions **1–17** by referring to the newspaper article on page **83**.

For questions **1–17**, answer by choosing from sections of the article (**A–E**) on page **83**. Some of the choices may be required more than once. Indicate your answers **on the separate answer sheet**.

Note: When more than one answer is required, these may be given **in any order**.

Which father or fathers

tries to avoid physical punishment?	**1**		
initially resented the restrictions of fatherhood?	**2**		
made a conscious decision to have a child?	**3**		
arranged his accommodation to be near his children?	**4**		
is involved in the children's daily routine?	**5**		
altered his professional duties to take account of his children?	**6**		
share interests with their children?	**7**	**8** ....
appreciated his children more as they grew older?	**9**		
treated his children as if they were grown up?	**10**		
doesn't force his children to maintain contact with him?	**11**		
was not as strict as his children would have wished?	**12**		
found his children's interests helped him with his job?	**13**		
had their children close together?	**14**	**15** ....
would have liked to attend more school events?	**16**		
did not want to repeat his parents' mistakes?	**17**		

FROM HERE TO PATERNITY

A The theatre director

'Because of my bizarre personal life, which I cannot be proud of, I have been blessed with 35 years of small children and I can honestly say I have loved every minute. I had the pleasure of feeding the baby this morning and that for me is what being a father is all about.

'I'm terribly lucky with my children. We all love the same things: opera, theatre, books, music. It creates a great bond, especially now that they are mostly grown up and I have become a friend rather than a father.

'I don't believe in physical violence. I have been guilty of slapping my children in anger, but I don't condone it. I'm sure I have not been a deeply attentive father but I have always tried to be available. I'm here if they need me, always on the basis that they ring me. As soon as you start chasing them to ask why they have not been in touch, you impose this terrible burden of guilt. My parents did it to me and I would never do it to my children.'

B The advertising executive

'I was young when they were born, only around 25, and I admit I found the responsibilities and limitations quite irksome. It aged me quickly, but at the same time it kept me young, which is something I have always valued.

'As they became teenagers, they introduced me to things I could have drifted away from: music, youth culture, clothes. In a funny way that has been invaluable as far as running the agency has been concerned. I have never felt out of touch.

'Because I was struggling to establish the business when they were young there were things I missed: first concerts, sports days. I'm sad about that, but there are compensations now, like being able to take them on holidays to the south of France.

'They get on well with a lot of our friends and they come to parties with us and advertising awards ceremonies without feeling intimidated. I think it has been an advantage that I do something they see as glamorous and interesting.'

C The politician

'My first child was born just as I was about to be elected onto the Greater London Council, and the others followed in quite quick succession. My wife and I vowed that we would carve out time for them but since I have become more and more politically active, time has become a real problem.

'I make it a condition that I will only accept weekend meetings and public appearances where there are facilities for one or more of the kids to come with me. If I did not they would just get squeezed out. This way they have a sense of what I do when I am not with them and there is no feeling of Daddy disappearing.

'I've noticed more and more MPs bringing their kids to the House. Maybe we are all becoming more conscious of the need to involve our children in our lives.'

D The writer

'My first marriage broke up when Kate and Bonnie were quite young, so I was forced to examine the whole area of fatherhood more closely than I might otherwise have done. I made enormous efforts to stay in touch with the children. My ex-wife and I even experimented with living next door to each other for a while, so they could come and go as they wished, but I think Kate and Bonnie would say now that they found that quite confusing.

'Kate has said in interviews that I was always there for her, but I am not sure I was a very good father. It is true I was around a lot, but, like a lot of Seventies parents, I think I treated the kids as adults too soon. Kate was complaining only the other day that we were too liberal. I think I could have introduced more systems, more order. Instead I took this very loose approach. I regret that now.

'I still worry about my elder daughters as much as I do about my youngest. In that way your kids never leave you.'

E The TV presenter

'I was ready for kids. I'd hit 30, met my wife, we had a lovely house, so we thought, "Why carry on going to the shops every Saturday spending our money on new sofas, when we could have a kid instead?"

'Having my daughter Betty has forced me to come to terms with who I am and what I am. You feel you are doing something very special when you conceive a child, and you are. But you are also becoming just one more parent in a great long line of parents. It's a great leveller.

'I do resent it occasionally but if ever there is a moment of irritation, it is dispelled by just one look at her. A baby's smile is the greatest self-preservation mechanism in the world. It can melt a grown man.'

Part 2

For questions **18–24**, choose which of the paragraphs **A–H** on page **85** fit into the numbered gaps in the magazine article below. There is one extra paragraph, which does not fit in any of the gaps.

Indicate your answers **on the separate answer sheet**.

THE DAY I GAVE UP SMOKING

I thought everyone would be pleased, but one of my colleagues was absolutely furious. 'What do you mean?' she raged. 'If it was that easy, why didn't you stop years ago?'

18	

The stop-smoking session was an interesting mixture of group therapy and hypnotherapy and it took place exactly two months and three weeks ago.

19	

On that unexceptional Thursday afternoon, I had simply gone along to the Birmingham session of *The Easy Way to Stop Smoking* to write an article about other people trying to give up. 'I shan't be trying to stop myself, it wouldn't be fair,' I announced firmly. 'Since my motivation for being here is writing, not stopping, it would not be right to expect your method to work on me.'

20	

We were encouraged to smoke as much as we wished and most of the afternoon was conducted in a room so smoke-filled that we had to open the windows.

21	

I suppose what happened was that the stop-smoking messages made intellectual sense. Just as smoking itself had become a challenge in the face of opposition, so the notion of stopping began to feel attractive.

22	

In many senses, it was easy. The physical craving, the pangs of desire for nicotine, in just the same place where you feel hunger, faded after a minute or two and I experienced them over only four or five days.

23	

Surprisingly, pottering around at home on weekend mornings proved to be the most difficult thing – and it still is.

24	

Yes, I *do* miss my cigarettes, but not too much. Each 'new' experience as a non-smoker has to be addressed – eating out, waiting for an aeroplane, booking into a hotel, a theatre interval. All are key moments in which I would have previously smoked cigarettes.

A The possibility of not being a smoker was beginning to make me feel powerful. It was a secret feeling that had nothing to do with anyone except myself. Could I also conquer the world?

B I suppose my inability to explain how one afternoon I had been a packet-a-day, life-long smoker, and four hours later I was not, was faintly irritating. I find it curious myself.

C I am increasingly coming to the view that for me smoking had a great deal to do with displacing boredom; having a cigarette was an activity in itself.

D I could not have been more reasonable. After all, I positively enjoyed smoking. It gave me real pleasure. I thought the counsellor looked at me rather knowingly.

E I had not intended to stop and I did not even particularly want to. For one thing, I wholly resented the remorseless pressure from the anti-smoking mob – and I still do. For another, I had low blood pressure and a long-living and healthy family. I did not cough or feel unwell and threw off colds more easily, it seemed to me, than friends with consciously healthier lifestyles.

F My skin is pinker, I can sing higher notes and I don't smell like a bonfire. People have stopped asking me if I have a sore throat.

G The one activity – my work – that I thought would be the most difficult to accomplish without cigarettes did not cause a single problem. I had really believed that I would not be able to work to deadlines unassisted by nicotine and that for the first time ever I would fail to write a story to order.

H I noticed with interest that when I was told to smoke I was reluctant to do so – and so were the others.

Part 3

Read the following article and answer questions **25–29** on page **87**. On your answer sheet, indicate the letter **A**, **B**, **C** or **D** against the number of each question. Give only one answer to each question.

Indicate your answers **on the separate answer sheet**.

Tapping into a food supply

In the forests of Madagascar there lives a primate with a lifestyle remarkably like a woodpecker's. Both the woodpecker and the primate, the rare and elusive aye-aye, bore through wood and probe cavities beneath the surface in their search for insect larvae. The woodpecker, of course, uses its beak for chiselling into the wood and its long tongue to extract its prey; the aye-aye, on the other hand, uses its incisor teeth to gnaw its way in and its narrow, elongated third finger to probe and scoop. Though the aye-aye's strange way of feeding was first described over a hundred years ago, scientists have only now discovered how it locates the insects hidden inside the wood.

Dr Carl Erickson, of Duke University's Primate Center, has been investigating the hunting skills of two captive males, Nosferatu and Poe, a female, Samantha, and her infant daughter, Annabelle (*Animal Behaviour*, vol. 41 pp. 793–802). He first tested whether they found insects just by looking for the telltale visual signs of their presence. For example, holes on the surface might indicate sites where female insects had entered the wood and laid their eggs. Dr Erickson presented the aye-ayes with logs in which he had drilled several narrow holes. Some holes led to cavities containing mealworms while others were blank dead-ends. The aye-ayes went straight for the cavities with food, gnawing through the wood and clearly not requiring the visual clues of surface holes.

Perhaps the aye-ayes were locating the mealworms by their smell or the sounds they were making. But further tests showed that they didn't use these clues either. Logs in which the smell of the insects was prevented from leaking out presented no problem, and the aye-ayes also located dead (and therefore silent) mealworms.

If they weren't seeing, smelling or hearing the insects, how were the aye-ayes able to find them? Dr Erickson discovered that they would gnaw down to empty cavities as well as those containing mealworms. They could apparently sense the cavity itself.

When searching for food, an aye-aye taps the surface of the wood with its middle finger and brings its exceptionally large ears forward, focusing them at a point in front of its nose. Dr Erickson suggests that the animal is echo-locating, listening and perhaps feeling for reverberations of the taps that indicate a hollow space below. It can probably also hear the rustle of insects, which might move when disturbed by the tapping from above.

The theory that the aye-aye takes the place of woodpeckers in the woodpecker-free forests of Madagascar is an attractive one. But there are birds, such as the Sickle-billed and Nuthatch Vangas, which do probe for or glean insects from wood, and so the woodpecker niche may not be vacant. Not only can the aye-aye be regarded as a woodpecker and an echo-locating bat rolled into one, but it also behaves like a squirrel (indeed, it was originally classified as one). Its incisors grow continuously like a squirrel's, and it has recently been observed in the wild gnawing through the shells of nuts, and extracting the meat of the nut with its elongated finger.

25 What do the woodpecker and the aye-aye have in common?
 A   They have exceptionally long tongues.
 B   They live in the same habitat.
 C   They have similar eating habits.
 D   They have strong beaks.

26 The aye-ayes studied by Dr Erickson
 A   were observed in their natural habitat.
 B   belonged to one family group.
 C   had been captured by hunters in Madagascar.
 D   lived in artificial conditions.

27 Dr Erickson's first hypothesis was that the aye-ayes
 A   were attracted to female insects and the eggs they laid.
 B   relied solely on visual senses to locate prey.
 C   were equally keen to investigate all cavities in wood.
 D   used their incisors to get faster access to food.

28 What was Dr Erickson's next hypothesis designed to test?
 A   the degree of development of the aye-aye's sense of touch
 B   the acuteness of the aye-aye's vision
 C   the keenness of the aye-aye's sense of hearing
 D   the role of smell in the aye-aye's search for food

29 Why was the aye-aye once considered to be a squirrel?
 A   It hoards nuts for the winter.
 B   It lives in trees.
 C   It has an unusual way of feeding.
 D   Its teeth don't stop growing.

Part 4

Answer questions **30–41** by referring to the reviews on pages **89–90**.

For questions **30–41**, answer by choosing from the reviews (**A–I**) on pages **89–90**. Some of the choices may be required more than once. Indicate your answers **on the separate answer sheet.**

Note: When more than one answer is required, these may be given **in any order.**

Which play is described as being

a change from the author's previous work?	**30**	
performed too infrequently?	**31**	
shorter than the original?	**32**	
almost a disaster?	**33**	
sometimes lacking in pace?	**34**	

Which production or productions provide an opportunity to see or hear

an action-packed performance?	**35**	
a highly-recommended comedy?	**36**	**37** ....
a newly-written work?	**38**	**39** ....
a mixture of sadness and comedy?	**40**	
a play about the role of women in society?	**41**	

THEATRE
CHARLES SPENCER

A Tamburlaine the Great

Marlowe's ten-act epic about the all-conquering warrior can seem never-ending, but it emerges as one of the most thrilling nights of the year in Terry Hands' staging. He has hacked great chunks from the text and offers a production that combines the glories of Marlowe's play with an exhilarating speed and physicality. Antony Sher is in terrific form in the title role, somersaulting from the balcony, sliding down a rope head-first as he delivers a speech, demanding and getting the audience's complete attention as his eyes glint with a mad lust for power and glory. Great stuff.

Swan Theatre, Stratford-upon-Avon (01789 295623)

B Women Laughing

Welcome London transfer for the late Michael Wall's fine play, seen at the Manchester Royal Exchange in May. The first act creates an atmosphere of unsettling menace as two married couples chat on a sunny suburban lawn. In the second half, the location shifts and the piece becomes a powerful, compassionate study of the devastating effects of illness. The British theatre lost a talent of great promise when Wall died at the tragically early age of 44.

Royal Court Theatre, London SW1 (0207 730 1745)

C Amphibians

Billy Roche is the latest in the long line of Irish dramatists to have enriched the English stage. All his plays to date have been set in his native Wexford, and this latest piece explores the decline of the fishing industry with his usual mixture of rich characterisation, painful emotion and sudden moments of quirky humour. The play sprawls a bit aimlessly at times, but builds to a blistering climax.

Barbican's Pit Theatre, London EC2 (0207 638 8891)

D Murder by Misadventure

Traditional thriller involving our old friend, 'the perfect murder'. This time it is Gerald Harper and William Gaunt who play the crime-writing partnership intent on killing each other, and though it's all rather familiar stuff, the twists and turns are handled with ingenuity.

Whitehall Theatre, London SW1 (0207 867 1119)

E The Alchemist

Young director Sam Mendes finds the gold in Jonson's great comedy of 17th-century confidence tricksters. First seen at the *Swan* in Stratford last year, the show works just as well on the Barbican's main stage, with Jonathan Hyde, David Bradley and Joanne Pearce repeating their fine performances as the wicked trio of con-artists.

Barbican Theatre, London EC2 (0207 638 8891)

F The Madras House

Peter James' production of Harley Granville Barker's rich, panoramic comedy about fashion and the position of women in Edwardian society transfers to London after its success at the Edinburgh Festival. The staging is stylish, the acting excellent, the play itself an unjustly neglected classic.

Lyric Theatre, Hammersmith, London W6 (0208 741 2311)

G Dreams from a summer house

This delightful new musical finds playwright Alan Ayckbourn in unusually benign form as he relocates the *Beauty and the Beast* story deep in the heart of London suburbia. A lush score by John Pattison and an unashamedly schmaltzy celebration of romantic love combine to make this good-hearted show a real winner. London impresarios looking for a hit should board the next train to Scarborough.

Stephen Joseph Theatre, Scarborough (01723 370541)

H The Merry Wives of Windsor

David Thacker's lacklustre production of Shakespeare's most farcical comedy came perilously close to being awarded the dreaded thumbs-down symbol, but this disappointing, crudely designed show is redeemed by first-rate comic performances from Ron Cook as the French physician Dr Caius and Anton Lesser as the explosively jealous husband, Ford. Almost everyone else looks faintly embarrassed, as well they might.

Shakespeare Theatre, Stratford-upon-Avon (01789 295623)

I The Voysey Inheritance

Another major Granville Barker revival, now touring the regions. This story of an apparently respectable solicitor who bequeaths a corrupt financial legacy to his son results in a marvellous play.

Apollo Theatre, Oxford (01865 244544)

PART 2: HARBOUR SCENES

Set of pictures (for Candidate A)

1.5C

1.5G

1.5D

1.5H

1.5E

1.5I

1.5F

1.5J

PART 2: HARBOUR SCENES

Set of pictures (for Candidate B)

1.5K

1.5O

1.5L

1.5P

1.5M

1.5Q

1.5N

1.5R

PART 2: PAST AND PRESENT

Set of pictures (for Candidates A and B)

1.5A

1.5B

PART 3: 'I could never…'

Set of pictures (for Candidates A and B)

PART 2: DIETS

Picture (for Candidates A and B)

2.5G

PART 2: DIETS

Picture (for Candidates A and B)

2.5H

PART 3: EDUCATION

Set of pictures (for Candidates A and B)

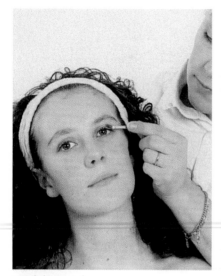

applying make-up

the environment

car maintenance

swimming

Mon	French	Geography	Maths	Sport	
Tues	English		History	Maths	Science
Wed	Geography	French		Cookery / Woodwork	
Thurs	History	Maths	English	Science	
Fri	Geography	Music	PE	History	Art

first aid

operating a computer

the Arts

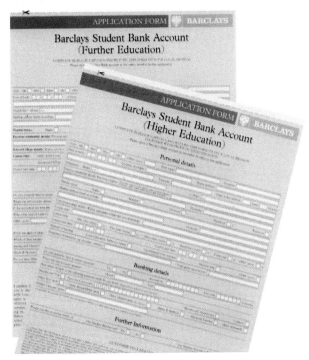

official forms

gardening

music

dancing

PART 2: HOLIDAY ACCOMMODATION

Set of pictures (for Candidates A and B)

2.5A

2.5B

2.5C

2.5D

2.5E

2.5F

PART 2: A ROOM OF YOUR OWN

Picture for Candidate A

3.5A

PART 2: A ROOM OF YOUR OWN

Picture for Candidate B

3.5B

PART 3: OLYMPIC SYMBOL

Set of pictures (for Candidates A, B and C)

PART 3: ENVIRONMENT COMPETITION

Set of pictures (for Candidates A, B and C)

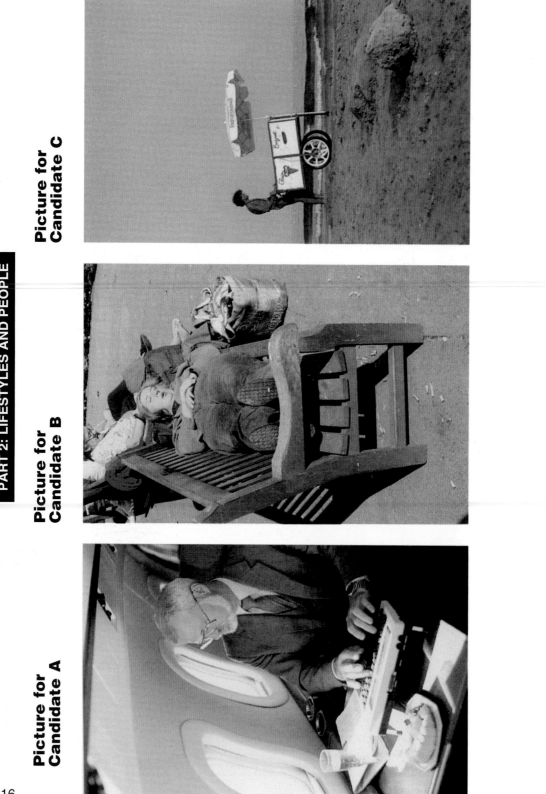

Picture for Candidate C

PART 2: LIFESTYLES AND PEOPLE

Picture for Candidate B

Picture for Candidate A

PAPER 2   WRITING (2 hours)

Part 1

You **must** answer this question.

1   You spent your last vacation acting as a team leader at a summer camp for young people in Canada. Other members of your English club are thinking of doing the same thing this year, and the secretary of the club has asked you to write a report based on your experiences and those of other team leaders so that new team leaders know what to expect.

Read the advertisement with your comments below and, on page **92**, the notes which you made after talking to other team leaders. Then, **using the information carefully**, write the **report**.

Canada Camp

Want to visit Canada but short of money?

Canada Camp **is the way to do it.**

We're looking for suitable people to work as team leaders
in camps throughout Canada.

We need people who:

including the camp leader – not easy!
get on with other people
are enthusiastic   *— and patience!*
have plenty of energy
swimming, climbing or riding essential
have skills they can pass on to others
love the countryside   *— wonderful scenery*
are looking for **adventure**

We offer:
no transport from airport to camp
return air ticket   *— dormitory with the kids*
meals and accommodation
pocket money   *— gained 3 kgs!*
the experience of a lifetime!

CANADA CAMP NOTES

1. Large group of kids, 8–12 years old – very different interests; not much time for self, sometimes felt more like school teacher – but a couple of the kids still keep in touch (J.B.)

2. 'Pocket money' was just that – not much use for seeing Canada afterwards; had to borrow from father (M.-J.C.)

3. Weather more changeable than expected – had to buy a raincoat! A few very hot days (P.D.)

4. Nearly had accident on the river – no-one trained to handle a canoe ... luckily Maria has life-saving certificate! An awful lot of responsibility really (T.L.S.)

5. Primitive conditions but a lot of fun – pity there was nowhere to buy film for my camera! (S.G.)

Now write the **report**. Your report should be about 250 words long.

Part 2

Choose **one** of the following writing tasks. Your answer should follow exactly the instructions given. Write approximately 250 words.

2 An increasing number of tourists are coming to visit your town. Your local tourist office is producing a series of leaflets to help tourists make the most of their visit. You have been asked to write a leaflet for visitors who have only a morning or afternoon to spend in your town.

Write the **leaflet**, recommending what they should do and why.

3 You recently attended a music festival or concert and want to write about it to an English-speaking friend who has the same or similar tastes as you. Write him/her a **letter** about the event and explain how it did or did not come up to your expectations.

Write your **letter**.

4 You have seen the following on your college notice-board:

THEFT is on the increase.
Have you got any ideas that will help students protect their personal property?
Your college magazine needs an article on this topic and is offering the latest Sherlock Holmes video for the best article.

Write the **article**, in which you put forward some suggestions on what students can do to protect their possessions.

5 A US company has asked you to write a brief practical **guide** to behaviour in business situations in your country. You should refer to appropriate ways of dressing, how to address people and how business people meet socially. Add any other comments on aspects of business behaviour in your country which you think would be useful.

Write the **guide**.

PAPER 3 ENGLISH IN USE (1 hour 30 minutes)

Part 1

For questions **1–15**, read the text below and then decide which word on page **95** best fits each space. Put the letter you choose for each question in the correct box on your answer sheet. The exercise begins with an example **(0)**.

Example:

0	A		0

CRIME – REVERSING THE TREND

Crime, as we are all **(0)** ... , has been a growing problem all over the world in the last thirty years. But we are not **(1)** ... against crime. Much is being done – and more can be done – to reverse the trend. You can play a part in it.

The first step towards preventing crime is understanding its **(2)** ... . Most crime is against property, not **(3)** ... , and most crime is not carried out by professionals; nor is it carefully planned. Property crimes **(4)** ... on the easy opportunity. They are often **(5)** ... by adolescents and young men, the majority of whom stop offending as they grow older – the **(6)** ... age for offending is fifteen. Also, and not surprisingly, the **(7)** ... of being a victim of crime **(8)** ... greatly depending on where you live.

This **(9)** ... by criminals on the easy opportunity is the **(10)** ... to much crime prevention. Motor cars, for example, are a sitting target for the criminal. Surveys have shown that approximately one in five drivers do not always **(11)** ... to secure their cars by locking all the doors and shutting all the windows, and in 30 per cent of domestic burglaries the burglar simply walks in without having to use **(12)** ... . If opportunities like these did not exist, criminals would have a much harder time. The chances are that many crimes would not be committed, which would release more police time for **(13)** ... serious crime.

Of course, the primary responsibility for **(14)** ... with crime rests with the police and the courts, but, if you care about improving the **(15)** ... of life for yourself and your community, there are many ways you can help reverse the trend.

0 (**A**) aware   **B** conscious   **C** informed   **D** known

1 A unprepared   **B** hopeless   **C** powerless   **D** weak

2 A nature   **B** type   **C** reason   **D** method

3 A the victim   **B** the public   **C** residents   **D** citizens

4 A increase   **B** thrive   **C** develop   **D** happen

5 A performed   **B** started   **C** committed   **D** done

6 A peak   **B** major   **C** maximum   **D** top

7 A percentage   **B** seriousness   **C** rate   **D** risk

8 A varies   **B** adapts   **C** transforms   **D** adjusts

9 A awareness   **B** seizing   **C** reliance   **D** taking

10 A answer   **B** method   **C** way   **D** key

11 A trouble   **B** bother   **C** care   **D** ensure

12 A force   **B** threat   **C** tools   **D** tricks

13 A removing   **B** facing   **C** tackling   **D** dealing

14 A containing   **B** destroying   **C** fighting   **D** coping

15 A quality   **B** peacefulness   **C** enjoyment   **D** way

Part 2

For questions **16–30**, complete the following article by writing each missing word in the correct box on your answer sheet. **Use only one word for each space**. The exercise begins with an example **(0)**.

Example:

0	providing	0

HERBS AND SPICES

There is nothing new in the use of herbs and spices. They have enriched human life for thousands of years, **(0)** ... both comfort and luxury. They have flavoured our food, cured our ailments and surrounded us **(16)** ... sweet scents. They have also played **(17)** ... part in our folklore and magic. It **(18)** ... be a very different world without them.

Nobody really knows who first used herbs and spices, or for **(19)** ... purpose. All their properties were known to the ancient Greeks and Egyptians and to **(20)** ... living in early Biblical times. The knowledge that they employed, and that we **(21)** ... use today, must have been based on the trial and error **(22)** ... early man, who was originally drawn to the plants **(23)** ... of their tantalising aroma. He gradually discovered their individual effects **(24)** ... his food and well-being and our use of them comes from those early experiments. For centuries herbs and spices were appreciated to the full but in modern times the arrival of **(25)** ... convenience foods and new medicines of the twentieth century almost **(26)** ... us forget them. But anything **(27)** ... has been so much loved and valued **(28)** ... never be completely neglected. The knowledge has been kept alive and **(29)** ... our present-day search **(30)** ... all things natural, herbs and spices have come into their own again.

Part 3

In **most** lines of the following text, there is **either** a spelling **or** a punctuation error. For each numbered line **31–46**, write the correctly spelled word or show the correct punctuation in the box on your answer sheet. **Some lines are correct.** Indicate these lines with a tick (✔) in the box. The exercise begins with three examples **(0)**, **(00)** and **(000)**.

Examples:

0	site	0
00	✔	0
000	officer, the	0

DEANSGATE

0	When Deansgate was a narrow street and the sight of Central Station
00	was a squalid slum, Wood Street Mission was founded. In 1869,
000	according to a contemporary police officer the neighbourhood was 'the
31	rendezvous of thieves, the worst haunt of vice. Meals were served
32	daily in the mission building to those who were hungry and thousand's
33	of pears of shoes were given away to those who arrived barefoot. At
34	Christmas four hundred tramps, and criminals came to a meal and a
35	religious service; in the summer children queud to be taken out for a
36	day at the seaside. Every single night the streets were searched for
37	homeless boys, who slept wherever they could, in door ways and
38	under market stalls. They were given beds in Wood Street. Jobs
39	were found for them and many were sent away to live in canada,
40	where most succeeded in creating new lives for themselfs. In 1892, a
41	new superintendent was appointed. He was an excriminal, and his
42	success was undoubtedly an inspiration to those he was trying to help.
43	His main acheivement was to create a holiday camp at a nearby
44	seaside resort wich could accommodate a hundred and twenty
45	children. Many local residence still remember happy holidays there.
46	The Mission still provides about a thousand familys a year with
	clothing and helps or advises many more.

Part 4

For questions **47–61**, read the two texts on pages **98** and **99**. Use the words in the boxes to the right of the texts to form **one** word that fits in the same numbered space in the text. Write the new word in the correct box on your answer sheet. The exercise begins with an example **(0)**.

Example: | 0 | readers | | 0 |

ADVERTISEMENT

TEN OUT OF TEN FOR OUR BEST EVER FICTION OFFER

We are delighted to offer all our **(0)** … our best bargain ever.
Featuring ten of today's most creative **(47)** … , this **(48)** …
selection of paperback fiction provides a unique opportunity to
catch up with what's hot in the world of literature. These books
are **(49)** … , thrilling and sometimes spine-chilling, providing
hours of **(50)** … for all the family. Ideal for sharing, this set could
also make ten **(51)** … and individual gifts. Each book would
normally cost at least £5.99 but you can enjoy the entire **(52)** …
for just £9.99 and save yourself an astonishing £53! Place your
order today to avoid **(53)** … .

(0)	READ
(47)	NOVEL
(48)	IMPRESS
(49)	HUMOUR
(50)	PLEASE
(51)	THOUGHT
(52)	COLLECT
(53)	DISAPPOINT

EXTRACT FROM ARTICLE

THE BRIGHTEST STAR

In the whole of the night sky, the brightest star is Sirius.
Otherwise known as the Dog Star, Sirius lies in the constellation
of Canis Major. Because of its **(54)** … in the sky, Sirius features
(55) … in ancient cultures and religions. Some Egyptologists
have even suggested that parts of the internal **(56)** … of the
pyramids have a specific **(57)** … to the position of Sirius in the
sky. In 1844, a German **(58)** … deduced from close **(59)** … that
Sirius was not alone. It 'wobbled' and this could only be due to
the **(60)** … of another star close by – its **(61)** … companion.
Sirius thus became the first known 'binary' or double star.

(54)	BRILLIANT
(55)	PROMINENCE
(56)	ARCHITECT
(57)	RELATION
(58)	ASTRONOMY
(59)	OBSERVE
(60)	PRESENT
(61)	VISIBLE

Part 5

For questions **62–74**, read the following teacher's comments on a school project. Use the information in it to complete the numbered gaps in the informal letter from the student who did the project. The words which you need **do not occur** in the teacher's comments. **Use no more than two words for each gap**. The exercise begins with an example **(0)**.

Example: | **0** | **to complete** | **0** |

TEACHER'S COMMENTS

CONTENT: Margaret's report on 'Language Development in Two-Year-Old Twins' represents a year's painstaking work. The case study shows various strengths, particularly acute observation but the material could have been more efficiently organised. The paper was perhaps over-ambitious since it extended to 10,000 words instead of the recommended 5,000.

STYLE: The writing is lively but too colloquial for this kind of text. Margaret is also sometimes inaccurate in her choice of vocabulary, with unfortunate results.

PRESENTATION: The project is pleasantly illustrated with photographs and some useful charts, though it is a pity these were not original. The work is marred by a number of typing and spelling errors and would have benefited from stricter proof-reading before submission.

INFORMAL LETTER

Dear Annie

How are you getting on with your language project? As you know, it took me a year (0) ... mine. And now I've just got a copy of the comments the teacher made on it, and she obviously thinks it's a bit of a disaster!

She seems quite (62) ... with my observations, but said the material could have been much (63) ... . I think that I probably (64) ... high because I (65) ... to 10,000 words when we were only (66) ... do 5,000. She certainly thought it was far (67) ... . Then she criticised me for using too much (68) ... and sometimes getting the (69) ... completely!

At least she (70) ... of the pictures I spent hours preparing (although she seemed to think I had (71) ... them!). But then she had a go at me about the number of (72) ... I made, and she obviously thinks these have (73) ... the whole project. I suppose the lesson to learn is that I should have let someone read it before I (74) ... it in.

Hope you have better luck than me.

Love, Margaret

Part 6

For questions **75–80**, read the following text and then choose from the list **A–J** given below the best phrase to fill each of the spaces. Write one letter (**A–J**) in the correct box on your answer sheet. Each correct sentence may only be used once. **Some of the suggested answers do not fit at all.** The exercise begins with an example **(0)**.

Example:

0	J		0

FINDING FISH

Fish are like any other living creature, in that they react in a number of different ways to the weather. The heat of the water in which they live **(0)** … are the two most important factors we have to consider when we try to find fish.

Fish can rise or sink into the deep water according to the temperature **(75)** … . They can also seek life-giving oxygen by moving closer to places that cause oxygen to be taken into the water such as waterfalls, fast-running streams and streams that run into a lake. Rainfall and wind sweeping across a lake also bring oxygen into the water, **(76)** … . Some fish do not need the same quantities of oxygen as others, so they are found in deep lakes **(77)** … . The trees drop an enormous number of leaves into the lake every winter. These decay, releasing dangerous gas.

In winter, we find that the warmest water is at the bottom of lakes and ponds. Fish tend to feed right at the bottom. Some stop feeding altogether as the cold months arrive, falling into a state of partial hibernation, **(78)** … . In summertime, we find a complete reversal of water temperature. The warmest water is just under the surface of the lake. As the depth becomes greater, so the water gets a lot colder. Fish that use little oxygen can rise to feed near the top of the water, **(79)** … .

Rivers are much less affected by hot weather. They are fed by water that seeps through the ground, **(80)** … and therefore not absorbing heat as still water does.

A   often surrounded by trees
B   constantly on the move
C   and generally they are swept across the lake to the windy side
D   that they find most comfortable
E   to be replaced by warmer water
F   coming out only on occasional sunny days
G   for warm water contains less oxygen than colder water
H   to the deeper parts of the lake
I   making the living conditions better for the inhabitants

J   and the amount of oxygen available to them

PAPER 4 LISTENING (approximately 45 minutes)

Part 1

You will hear part of a radio programme on food. Janet, a journalist who specialises in cookery, is giving a talk about bread. For questions **1–10**, complete the notes.

You will hear the recording **twice**.

AMOUNT OF BREAD EATEN

Last year consumption [**1**] by [**2**]

In previous ten years consumption [**3**]

by [**4**] per cent

OTHER CHANGES

Bread was made with bleached flour.

Is now often made with [**5**] flour.

Change because people believe this is [**6**]

Influences on tastes are [**7**] and [**8**]

Ingredients in bread making

rye flour
[**9**]
[**10**]
softened grains

Part 2

You will hear an introduction to a course in Business Management Today. For questions **11–21**, complete the information.

Listen very carefully as you will hear the recording ONCE only.

BUSINESS MANAGEMENT TODAY

Seminar/Workshop Programme

MARKETING			**11**

	12	Bishop's Hall One
STRATEGIC PLANNING		Bishop's Hall Two

HUMAN RESOURCES		**13**

TIMETABLE	*LOCATION*	
9.30 – 11.30	Convocation Hall	
Coffee and biscuits		**14**
11.30 – 1.00		**15**
Lunch		**16**
2.00 – 3.30 Tea and biscuits		**17**
4.00 – 5.30		**18**
5.30 – 6.30		**19**

NB Books and resource materials

on display in		**20**
Centre closes		**21**

Part 3

You will hear part of a radio programme for university students. For questions **22–28**, choose the correct answer **A, B, C** or **D**.

You will hear the recording **twice**.

22 Tony's ideal job would be as a TV presenter because he thinks
    A   he would meet interesting people.
    B   it would suit his personality.
    C   he would enjoy the fame.
    D   it would be an easy job.

23 He thinks that he won't get his ideal job because
    A   he is more suited to something else.
    B   he lacks the ambition required for it.
    C   he would face too much competition for it.
    D   he lacks the talent required for it.

24 He wouldn't consider working abroad because he
    A   would miss too many things.
    B   lacks ability at languages.
    C   would find it hard to get work abroad.
    D   lacks the courage to do it.

25 He feels that the course has been good because
    A   it has been very practical.
    B   it has taught him discipline.
    C   the work has been stimulating.
    D   he has received individual help.

26 He thinks that his future earnings
    A   will start low but improve.
    B   are not important to him.
    C   will be lower than they should be.
    D   will never be very high.

27 What will he miss most about being a student?
    A   the social life
    B   the lack of responsibility
    C   the irregular hours
    D   the people he has met

28 What will he miss least?
    A   the hard work
    B   the living conditions
    C   the lectures
    D   the gossip

Part 4

You will hear five short extracts in which different people say what they attribute their success to. For questions **29–38**, choose the correct answer **A, B** or **C**.

You will hear the recording **twice**.

29 The **first speaker** says his success is due to
   A determination.
   B luck.
   C family tradition.

30 What does he believe his success produced?
   A problems at home
   B a sense of achievement
   C other people's respect

31 The **second speaker** says her success is due to
   A help from her family.
   B talent.
   C hard work.

32 For her, the reward of success has been
   A financial security.
   B fame.
   C assisting others.

33 The **third speaker** attributes her success to
   A her parents' encouragement.
   B a chance meeting.
   C her school interests.

34 The best thing about her job is
   A meeting the patients.
   B the responsibility.
   C her boss.

35 The **fourth speaker** attributes his success to
   A maturity.
   B determination.
   C childhood ambition.

36 The cause of his changing career was
   A personal dissatisfaction.
   B a piece of bad luck.
   C a generous offer.

37 The **fifth speaker** attributes her success to
   A planning.
   B luck.
   C endurance.

38 What satisfies her most about her present work?
   A working for TV
   B international travel
   C working in a team

PAPER 5   SPEAKING (15 minutes)

There are two examiners. One (the interlocutor) conducts the test, providing you with the necessary materials and explaining what you have to do. The other examiner (the assessor) will be introduced to you, but then takes no further part in the interaction.

Part 1 (3 minutes)
The interlocutor will first ask you and your partner a few questions. You will then be asked to find out some information about each other, on topics such as hobbies, interests, career plans, etc.

Part 2 (4 minutes)
You will each be given the opportunity to talk for about a minute, and to comment briefly after your partner has spoken.

   The interlocutor gives you a set of pictures and asks you to talk about them for about one minute. Each set of pictures has a different focus, so it is important to listen carefully to the interlocutor's instructions. The interlocutor then asks your partner a question about your pictures and your partner responds briefly.

   You will then be given another set of pictures to look at. Your partner talks about these pictures for about one minute. This time the interlocutor asks you a question about your partner's pictures and you respond briefly.

Part 3 (4 minutes)
In this part of the test you and your partner will be asked to talk together. The interlocutor will place a new set of pictures on the table between you. This stimulus provides the basis for a discussion. The interlocutor will explain what you have to do.

Part 4 (4 minutes)
The interlocutor will ask some further questions, which will lead to a more general discussion of what you have talked about in Part 3. You will be encouraged to comment on what your partner says, and the interlocutor will also take part in the discussion.

Test 1 Key

Paper 1 Reading (1 hour 15 minutes)

Part 1

1 E   2 E   3 B   4 A   5 B/D   6 D/B   7 B   8 D
9 E   10 C/E   11 E/C   12 D   13 A   14 C

Part 2

15 C   16 B   17 G   18 F   19 E   20 A

Part 3

21 B   22 C   23 C   24 D   25 D   26 D

Part 4

27 C/D   28 C/D   29 C/D   30 C/D   31 D   32 G
33 D/E   34 D/E   35 D   36 B/G   37 B/G   38 A
39 A/E/F   40 A/E/F   41 A/E/F   42 H

Paper 2 Writing (2 hours)

Part 1

Question 1

Content (points covered)
(a) All relevant points as in rubric and Malcolm's letter, i.e.:
     Malcolm not the mugger;
     Malcolm not an American tourist;
     Malcolm injured;
     thief not caught;
     plus request for letter/corrections to be printed.
(b) Description of action taken, and expression of sympathy.

Organisation and cohesion
(a) Correct letter format with clear paragraphs and appropriate introductory
     reference to original article. Cohesive devices used effectively to link the
     details of the incident and the request for corrections.
(b) Well-balanced – succinct emphasis on relevant action taken but also brief
     social language, a clear development using appropriate cohesive devices.

Range
Shows clear contrast in expression between (a) and (b). Minimal lifting from
the question paper, some paraphrasing.

(a) The field of newspapers.
(b) Friendly reassurance.

Register
(a) Formal indignation, i.e. polite.
(b) Friendly/informal.

Target reader
(a) Newspaper editor would be persuaded to publish the letter, from which an accurate picture of what happened would emerge.
(b) Malcolm would be reassured.

Part 2

Question 2

Content (points covered)
How TV works.
Number of channels and what they are like.
Recommendations and reasons.
Any programme(s) to avoid and reasons.
Recognition of fact that person is not fluent in writer's language.

Organisation and cohesion
The two parts of the task – instructions and advice – must be clearly laid out; two well-constructed paragraphs or a series of short paragraphs would be equally effective.
Cohesive devices particularly important in advising on choice of programmes.

Range
Two different types of expression: instructional language and advice on programmes.
Correct use of 'technical' vocabulary, e.g. 'remote control'.
Reasonably sophisticated expansion of reasons for advice given, i.e. not just 'boring' or 'nice'.

Register
Informal to friendly.

Target reader
The friend from abroad will know what to do and have a clear idea of what to watch suited to language and own interests.

Question 3

Content (points covered)
Differentiation between *status* and *care* of elderly in own community.
How changed over last 50 years.
Developments writer would like to see in future (should be 'anchored' geographically).

Organisation and cohesion
Appropriate paragraphing with a clear introduction and conclusion.
Effective linking of the changes and the suggested developments.

Range
Expressions of process and change rather than present situation only.
Interesting opening with some original language.
Command of relevant vocabulary, e.g. old people's home, the state, etc.

Register
Fairly formal – not explicitly polemical.

Target reader
Readers of international magazine would be informed and interested.

Question 4
Content (points covered)
Some reference to the desert island/competition context.
Three books described clearly.
For each book, an explanation of why the book is important to the candidate.

Organisation and cohesion
Three books should be given reasonably equal weight; a purposeful opening
and brief conclusion.
Cohesive connection of description of each book and why it is important to the
candidate.

Range
Competent use of both factual language and the language of personal opinion.
(The language of literary criticism is not expected.)
Ability to summarise, describing clearly what each book is about.

Register
Neutral – but some enthusiasm evident, with a touch of rhetoric.

Target reader
Judges of competition should be impressed enough to award candidate a prize.

Question 5
Content (points covered)
How company recruits new staff.
How it trains new staff.
Training for existing staff.

Organisation and cohesion
Suitable report layout.
Could have sub-headings or be presented in continuous prose. Short
introduction and conclusion aimed at the target reader indicate good
planning.

Range
Some evidence of specialist vocabulary, e.g. personnel; training courses; diplomas etc.

Register
Formal; (shouldn't make assumptions about readers' knowledge of the world of work; a 'user-friendly' delivery is required).

Target reader
Students should have clear picture which is not too specialised.

Paper 3 English in Use (1 hour 30 minutes)

(1 mark for each correct answer)

Part 1

1 C (understand)   2 B (hunted for)   3 A (act)   4 D (leads)
5 B (day)   6 B (urge)   7 C (appearing)   8 D (outdoor)
9 A (suitable)   10 B (meant)   11 D (produced)   12 D (final)
13 C (materials)   14 A (destroyed)   15 D (distances)

Part 2

16 more   17 by   18 of   19 until/till   20 across/upon
21 as   22 another   23 from   24 but/although/though
25 to   26 There   27 these   28 into   29 their   30 less/not

Part 3

31 they   32 had   33 was   34 ✓   35 goes   36 ✓   37 a
38 to   39 as   40 ✓   41 well   42 ✓   43 of   44 ✓
45 very   46 up

Part 4

47 colourful   48 daily   49 refreshments   50 development(s)
51 paintings   52 unusual   53 fascinating
54 careless   55 avoidable   56 reasonably   57 incorrectly
58 injury/injuries   59 loosening   60 steadily   61 necessity

Part 5

62 vacancies/openings   63 advised/encouraged   64 present/the moment
65 in medicine   66 much appreciate/welcome/value   67 graduate
68 experience of   69 accept/undertake   70 well paid
71 enclose/attach/include   72 recent   73 details
74 contacted/reached

Part 6

75 G　　76 B　　77 H　　78 E　　79 D　　80 F

Paper 4 Listening (45 minutes)

Part 1

1 ✗　　2 ✓　　3 ✓　　4 ✓　　5 ✓　　6 ✓　　7 ✗　　8 ✗　　9 ✗
10 ✓　　11 ✗　　12 ✗　　13 ✓　　14 ✗　　15 ✗　　16 ✓　　17 ✗
18 ✓

Part 2

19 Divisional Director　　20 Plastic Magic
21 questions　　22 assembly line(s)　　23 seminar
24 admin(istrative) section　　25 Personnel Director

Part 3

26 3 years ago　　27 4.30　　28 hell　　29 salt
30 properly/perfectly/consistently/right/exactly　　31 pressure　　32 team
33 competing/racing　　34 staff/personality problems *or* accounts
35 accounts *or* staff/personality problems
36 self-promotion/promoting/selling/pushing themselves/PR

Part 4

37 D　　38 B　　39 F　　40 A　　41 E
42 D　　43 H　　44 F　　45 E　　46 C

Transcript　　*This is the Cambridge Certificate in Advanced English Listening Test. Test One.*

This paper requires you to listen to a selection of recorded material and answer the accompanying questions.

*There are four parts to the test, **One**, **Two**, **Three** and **Four**. You will hear Part Two **once** only. All the other parts of the test will be heard twice.*

There will be a pause before each part to allow you to look through the questions, and other pauses to let you think about your answers. At the end of every pause you will hear this sound.

tone

*You should write your answers on the **question** paper. You will have **ten** minutes at the end to **transfer your answers to the separate answer sheet**.*

The tape will now be stopped. You must ask any questions now as you will not be allowed to speak during the test.

[pause]

PART 1   *Now open your question paper and look at Part One.*

[pause]

Part One

You will hear a news report about storm damage in three regions, the South West, the South East and the North. The effects of this damage are listed. For questions 1 to 18, put a tick in the box to indicate what has happened in each region. If nothing has happened, put a cross. You will hear the recording twice.

[pause]

tone

Presenter: ... and now to the main news, namely last night's storm damage. People awoke this morning to face a massive clearing-up operation after torrential rains and hurricane force winds swept the entire country overnight leaving a trail of devastation in their wake. For news on the current situation we go over to our regional studios to hear from our reporters on the spot. And over to you Chris Baldwin in the South West.

Chris Baldwin: The South West has seen the worst flooding in thirty years with whole villages cut off, and many people still trapped in their homes by rising flood waters. Storm force waves have broken the sea wall at Westlington and it is feared that an entire lifeboat crew lost their lives in attempting to rescue the sailors on board a capsized trawler. Once weather conditions improve, the air-sea rescue forces will start a search for survivors but hopes of finding anyone alive are considered remote. In the meantime, emergency services are doing their best to restore power lines and rescue people and farm animals trapped in outlying areas, but police and firemen are hampered by appalling weather conditions. Now over to Harry Murdoch in the South East.

Harry Murdoch: And in the South East the picture is much the same with all train services into the capital suspended until further notice. Road transport is also disrupted by storm damage and people have been warned to stay away from town centres where many buildings are in danger of collapse. Trees have been blown down or uprooted and in some cases water and gas mains have burst, creating even more danger. Firemen have evacuated many people whose houses were destroyed and I am told that the cost of the damage to homes alone runs into many millions. And now over to Lily Normington in the North.

Lily Normington: I'm afraid the situation in the North is very serious indeed. A number of people have been killed by falling debris and in some cases are feared to be trapped in cars which have been crushed by falling trees. During the night the river Tone burst its banks sweeping away the main road and rail bridges across the river. Ships have been torn from their moorings and people have been warned to stay well away from the river banks. Reports are coming in of roads completely blocked by high-sided vehicles which have overturned, making it impossible for emergency services to get through. A number of people ...

[pause]

tone

Now you will hear the recording again.

[The recording is repeated.]

[pause]

That is the end of Part One.

[pause]

PART 2

Part Two
You will hear part of a telephone conversation in which a secretary is noting down details of an Open Day programme. For questions 19 to 25, complete the notes. Listen very carefully as you will hear the recording ONCE only.

[pause]

tone

Jenny: (*Phone being picked up, dialling.*) Hi, Meg? Jenny here. … Have you got the details for the Open Day programme yet? I've got to get them typed up by tomorrow … Yeah, oh fine. So, I've got 'Arrival 9.30', who's doing the welcome? Jim? … OK, I'll just put … 'Divisional Director', yeah? … Then they have the film, at a quarter to ten, which one? … 'Plastic Magic!' Who thinks up these titles? … And what follows that? The tour? …Oh, I see, so I put 'followed by questions', yeah? So they realise. *Then* the tour of the assembly lines, right? … Then at eleven I suppose it's what Jim insists we call a 'seminar' on our career structure? … Well I think 'seminar' sounds so pretentious! … Well, no doubt, but anyway, what's next? Oh yes, 'visit to the Administrative Section' at twelve. What's happening about lunch for them? … So I'll just say, thirteen hundred, lunch with Administrative, no sorry, Personnel, of course, Personnel Director, fourteen hundred depart, right? … Sure.

So, let me check, I've got to remind the Divisional Director about his welcome talk, make sure the foreman knows they'll be visiting the assembly line at half past ten, *and* make sure Jim knows he's got to finish his 'seminar' on time so they'll have a clear hour with the admin. people. OK? … Fine. Thanks, 'bye. (*Phone replaced.*)

[pause]

tone

That is the end of Part Two.

[pause]

PART 3

Part Three
You will hear a radio interview with a young woman who runs her own restaurant. For questions 26 to 36, complete the sentences. You will hear the recording twice.

[pause]

tone

Susie: Now establishing and running your own restaurant is a daunting prospect for even an experienced chef. Christine Patterson has done it in only three years and at the age of twenty-six. In the third in our series on successful chefs, Terry Brownjohn visited Christine in her restaurant, 'The Torn Curtain' in Great Malvern. After leaving a general catering college course Christine then started working for a rather well-known chef.

Christine: I began working for Tom Payne in the patisserie. Starting at four-thirty in the morning I wasn't exactly at my best and the first six months were hell. I was put on the croissant section and I used to weigh up ten kilos of dough, make them and then think, 'Did I actually put the salt in there or did I not?' and of course you never found out till the next morning at four thirty when the chef opened the prover door.

Terry: Sorry, what's the prover?

Christine: It's the place where you leave the croissants to rise before you cook them. (Ah!) So, there I was, opening the prover door the next day and there were a thousand croissants sitting looking exactly the same as they did the night before and on several occasions I was lifted up by my chef's jacket and told that if I got it wrong one more time then I'd be out and suddenly I realised perfection, consistency, standards were really the art of the day.

Terry: How old were you at the time you were there?

Christine: I was twenty when I started there. When I started at the patisserie there were three of us and the chef used to feel rather proud of this that we actually managed to run the whole croissant section on our own and it became a bit like a circus act. Whenever a friend of Tom's used to come in he used to introduce us and tell his friend how old we were and how long we had worked for him and it was obviously some great feat that three girls could work in one kitchen at one time.

Terry: And, um, what did you do after that?

Christine: From the patisserie I went to 'The Gaiety', which, yes, it was a nightmare for six months because the pressure's on, not just from the chef but from everybody else. It's a big team and you've just got to pull your weight. If one person mucks up one thing from overcooking the carrots, that will ruin the dish of the day so the top person gets told off and it just goes down the line. And the pressure and the speed was on. You had to do everything as fast as possible and to do that you used to work by the clock. You used to race each other. I used to have to do things like peeling large prawns. I used to have a dustbin load that I'd have to do and each day I would time myself to see how long I could do it in. I could do it in twenty minutes, fifteen minutes, ten minutes and then you'd find that the chef you were working with could do it in eight minutes so then you started again and thought right I can beat him. I'm a woman but I'm the same.

Terry: So it sounds like an endurance test. Was it?

Christine: Well, I think it is an endurance test, yes, and I feel now that because you've worked under such pressure but you can still produce top quality food, that whatever happens to me now I can manage to go into this overdrive facility whether I've got no energy or whatever I can still produce what I want to do.

Terry: And how have you found it, running your own restaurant?

Christine: Been running my own restaurant now for nearly three years and so far so good, yes it's been hard work and I've learnt more again on the managing side of things. I've never really had to deal with staff when there are problems – you know – personality clashes, people getting upset and then it ends up with you, you give them the final answer and you're meant to know everything there and then. I also never have been involved in the accounts. You think twice if something is more than seven pounds a pound because you really have to work out whether you really can use it. I think the sad thing is you often find that people are more conservative than you had hoped.

Terry: You're one of the few successful women in catering. Why do you think women aren't better known in your field?

Christine: Yes, yes, indeed. I think there are a lot of women in catering but sadly, they don't promote themselves, they don't push themselves. I see my restaurant and my cooking as a product, and as with any product you have to promote it, you have to push it. You have to do PR and you have to sell it and sadly I think there are a lot of women who run a good restaurant, who do very good food but that's it. Every male chef I've ever met is very forward, he thinks what he does is fantastic, he thinks he runs the best restaurant.

[pause]

tone

Now you will hear the recording again.

[The recording is repeated.]

[pause]

That is the end of Part Three.

[pause]

PART 4

Part Four
You will hear five short extracts in which people talk about various objects.
Task One. For questions 37 to 41, match the extracts as you hear them with the pictures labelled A to H.
Task Two. For questions 42 to 46, match the extracts as you hear them with the purposes listed A–H.
You will hear the recording twice. While you listen you must complete both tasks.

[pause]

tone

Customer: Now, price isn't a problem, but I must be able to use it underwater down to about 50 metres …

Salesman: Well, this one here fits the bill very well sir.

Customer: But can you make precise timings, down to an accuracy of a tenth of a second, at least?

Salesman: Ah, not on this one, no, sir. But this one here would suit you …

Man: I can't get it open!

Woman: Just slide back this little catch. Like this … Oh, it must be jammed. I wonder why that is.

Man: I don't know.

Woman: Have you wound it back?

Man: No. I thought that was automatic.

Woman: Well, it is, as a matter of fact. I meant, has it wound back?

Man: Well, no.

Woman: So that just means you haven't finished. You can still take another one or two.

Salesman:	How about these then?
Woman:	Oh, I've a friend who says the blades stay sharp forever. Is that so?
Salesman:	Yes, they're made of carbon fibre.
Woman:	Well, I'm none the wiser.
Salesman:	Well, nobody's ever been back to complain. I've sold several pairs to dressmakers and tailors.
Woman:	Um. How much are they?
Youth:	It sounds terrific; really great! And it'll find the right track for you – without any help?
Salesman:	If you like, yes. It's a big advantage.
Youth:	I like the black finish.
Salesman:	Everybody seems to.
Woman:	You can do all sorts of things with it. Look, it's designed so that you use it pointing straight ahead, and if you use it like that, it's phenomenally bright. It really blinds you if you look straight into that! Look.
Man:	Yes. Hey! don't do that!
Woman:	Sorry. You can hang it up, too, like this. I'm really pleased with it. Only £12.99. Brilliant value.
Man:	True.

[pause]

tone

Now you will hear the recording again.

[The recording is repeated.]

[pause]

*That is the end of Part Four. There will now be a ten minute pause to allow you to **transfer your answers to the separate answer sheet**. Be sure to follow the numbering of all the questions. The question papers and answer sheets will then be collected by your supervisor.*

Teacher, pause the tape here for ten minutes. Remind your students when they have one minute left.

That is the end of the test.

Test 2 Key

Paper 1 Reading (1 hour 15 minutes)

Part 1

1 F   2 A   3 G   4 C   5 H   6 I   7 D   8 E
9 B   10 C   11 F   12 G   13 B   14 I

Part 2

15 E   16 D   17 F   18 A   19 G   20 C

Part 3

21 C   22 C   23 A   24 D   25 B

Part 4

26 C   27 A   28 B   29 D   30 E   31 D   32 G   33 F
34 G   35 C   36 E   37 F   38 B   39 G   40 D   41 G

Paper 2 Writing (2 hours)

Part 1

Question 1

Content (points covered)
(a) Do not want to proceed with loan request.
(b) Thanks for suggestion about aunt; description of action proposed.
(c) Introduction of self; clear explanation of why letter is being written;
     request for some appropriate help – information or meeting, perhaps;
     reference to aunt as expert in field.

Organisation and cohesion
All three come to point quickly. Organisation or cohesion skills most likely to
be evident in (c).

Range
Wide range of vocabulary, structure (in particular use of tenses).

Register
(a) Formal, impersonal response to query in postcard.
(b) Informal, friendly thanks.
(c) Formal, respectful, tactfully persuasive polite request.

Target reader
In (a) and (c) will understand exactly what is expected of them; (b) will be
pleased that her information has been acted upon; (c) will be willing to help.

Part 2

Question 2

Content (points covered)
Some advice – a clear choice of one of the three options in the letter. At least
some reference to the other options and why they are less suitable in the
writer's opinion. Some friendly remarks outside the main point of the letter.

Organisation and cohesion
Appropriate opening and closing remarks for an informal letter.

Range
Demonstrates some structures appropriate to giving advice.

Register
Informal, friendly.

Target reader
Has a clear idea of what their friend is recommending.

Question 3

Content (points covered)
Refers to a number of free and/or inexpensive activities. Is of particular
relevance to students.

Organisation and cohesion
Attracts reader's attention in the opening sentence. Finishes on a strong note.
Any appropriate format acceptable.

Range
An interesting article will use a range of structures and the vocabulary chosen
will not be monotonous.

Register
Neutral or informal.

Target reader
Would have some good ideas of things to do that will not be expensive.

Question 4

Content (points covered)
Brief greeting to friend.
Explanation regarding next-door neighbour – who, how old, etc.
Should mention that the person is 'difficult'.
Outline of problems and what friend should do.

Organisation and cohesion
Set of clear notes or brief paragraphs.
NB   Short form notes are acceptable.

Range
Language of suggestion and advice.
Vocabulary relating to care/elderly.

Register
Informal, friendly tone.

Target reader
Friend should understand the situation and have lots of ideas of what to do.

Question 5

Content (points covered)
Reason for writing.
Reference to where the advert was seen.
Some basic (concrete) information to support application.
Mention of referees.
Making it clear that they are applying for a job, not a free holiday.

Organisation and cohesion
Laid out in clear paragraphs – at least three.

Range
Structures and vocabulary appropriate to a formal letter of application –
appropriate use of expressions like 'I look forward to hearing from you', 'I
enclose the names and addresses of two referees', 'I had some experience of
similar work when . . .', 'With reference to the advertisement for a housesitter
in yesterday's Times', etc.

Register
Formal.

Target reader
Would take the application reasonably seriously.

Paper 3 **English in Use** (1 hour 30 minutes)

(1 mark for each correct answer)

Part 1

1 A (world)	2 B (persuade)	3 C (develop)	4 D (having)
5 C (good)	6 A (validity)	7 A (contain)	8 B (fighting)
9 D (produce)	10 C (healing)	11 D (sign)	12 B (rid)
13 B (waste)	14 A (consider)	15 D (called)	

Part 2

16 being   17 at   18 that/which   19 by/in/as   20 have
21 them   22 do/can/may   23 just/only   24 a   25 either
26 are   27 for   28 be   29 something   30 for

Part 3

31 a   32 ✓   33 of   34 been   35 as   36 to   37 did
38 from   39 at   40 ✓   41 was   42 ✓   43 it   44 ✓
45 for   46 some

Part 4

47 loyalty   48 successful   49 objective(s)   50 demanding
51 freedom   52 rapidly   53 conferences   54 creature
55 instinctively   56 dependent   57 inappropriately   58 healthy
59 uncommon   60 researchers   61 investigations

Part 5

62 opening time   63 delay/wait
64 no apology/no explanation/no excuse
65 manner/behaviour/attitude/conduct/language
66 as smart/as neat/as tidy/as clean
67 admission charge/entrance charge/entrance fee   68 lit
69 half/fifty per cent/five/50%   70 of order/of action
71 missing from/absent from/lacking from
72 not available/unavailable/not served
73 stale/not fresh   74 catering

Part 6

75 A   76 B   77 F   78 I   79 C   80 E

Paper 4 Listening (45 minutes)

Part 1

1 5–0   2 4–1   3 5–0   4 3–1   5 2–0   6 no   7 B
8 wrist injury   9 3

Part 2

10 Station Hotel   11 laundry charges   12 daily travel/transport
13 lunch   14 excess luggage/baggage   15 £943   16 £500
17 12 weeks/3 months   18 overseas applicants/people from abroad
19 10 weeks

Part 3

20 B   21 A   22 C   23 D   24 D   25 C

Part 4

26 A   27 B   28 A   29 B   30 B
31 C   32 C   33 A   34 C   35 B

Transcript   *This is the Cambridge Certificate in Advanced English Listening Test. Test Two.*

This paper requires you to listen to a selection of recorded material and answer the accompanying questions.

*There are four parts to the test, **One, Two, Three** and **Four**. You will hear Part Two **once** only. All the other parts of the test will be heard twice.*

There will be a pause before each part to allow you to look through the questions, and other pauses to let you think about your answers. At the end of every pause you will hear this sound.

tone

*You should write your answers on the **question** paper. You will have **ten** minutes at the end to **transfer your answers to the separate answer sheet**.*

The tape will now be stopped. You must ask any questions now as you will not be allowed to speak during the test.

[pause]

PART 1   *Now open your question paper and look at Part One.*

[pause]

Part One
You will hear a recording of a radio sports report. For questions 1 to 9, complete the notes. You will need to write a number, a letter or a few words. You will hear the recording twice.

[pause]

tone

Presenter: In five minutes the weather and travel city by city. Now, sports news with Carol Findlay.

Carol: Good morning. Peter Gordon has stolen the headlines again after scoring four goals in England's five–nil defeat of South Korea in the second round of the World Cup Competition. Fellow England player Graham Lasky got the fifth goal. Elsewhere the cupholders Germany scored three goals in the last fifteen minutes to beat Costa Rica four–one. Holland beat the USA five–nil, and Argentina scored two late goals to beat Austria three–one. Two players were sent off in Italy's two–nil defeat of Lithuania, Roberto Rinaldi and Petris Kezys both taking early showers.

On to boxing now. The manager of British heavyweight Barry Jason has played down reports that he's to fight Mexican Manuel Fernandez next year. Fernandez, who beat Rocky Cavallini at the London Arena on Tuesday said he'll fight Jason early next year but Jason's manager Dicky Clough said the fight is unlikely to take place.

In golf, Bruce Chappell defends his European Open title at the St Andrew's course in Scotland. Carrying the Australian's golf clubs for him today will be 18-year-old Philip Johnston, the Junior Champion at St Andrew's. Christian Bernhardt misses that tournament because of a wrist injury but you can hear full reports from St Andrew's throughout the day here on Radio 5.

Tennis. World number one Marina Stieff has entered the Midland Bank Tournament at Brighton later this month. She'll be aiming for a record-breaking fourth triumph and is already favourite to take the first place.

Presenter: Thank you, Carol. You're listening to 'Morning Edition' on Radio 5 – the time is eleven minutes past eight.

[pause]

tone

Now you will hear the recording again.

[The recording is repeated.]

[pause]

That is the end of Part One.

[pause]

PART 2

Part Two
You will hear the chairperson of the Technological Society making an announcement at the end of a meeting. For questions 10 to 19, complete the information sheet. You will need to write a number or a few words. Listen very carefully as you will hear the recording ONCE only.

[pause]

tone

Chairperson: ... I know that many of you have trains to catch and in a couple of cases flights to catch so I won't keep you very much longer. However, you are aware that the sheet listing course dates, fees and other information which was sent out prior to this meeting was incomplete. I'm afraid not all the details had been confirmed by the time we went to press and there are a number of omissions. However, I'm now in a position to give you the rest of this information so you can add it to your copy.

We've been fortunate in obtaining the same hotel as last year – that's the Station for the people on attachment so the residential periods will be spent at the Station Hotel in Brimston Square. The overall fee will now include laundry charges. I know that there were disagreements last year as it was felt that costs of personal laundry while away from home should not be borne by participants. However, you will still need funds to cover your daily travel costs from the hotel to the training centre and although the hotel will provide breakfast and evening meal you will need to meet both transport as I've just mentioned and, er, lunch each day out of your own pocket. You may remember, however, that subsidised lunches are available at the training centre so they won't be too expensive.

For those of you travelling from abroad I should also point out that the Society is not in a position to help with any charges for excess baggage. The standard allowance as you know is twenty kilos and if you have bought books, gifts or whatever to take home with you, any additional costs are your responsibility.

You will be pleased to learn that the fees for the *Industrial Relations* course have stayed the same as last year – so that's £943. Unfortunately, though, the fees for the *Management Today* course have not yet been finalised; they will vary from last year but you might like to know that they will be approximately somewhere in the region of £500. I'm sure it won't have escaped your attention that we failed to print the length of each course. The *Industrial Relations* course is a twelve-week course as is *Management Today* – both three months as usual.

The two charges listed under the *Training Officers'* course apply to members of the Society and those who are eligible for awards or scholarships. The lower figure applies to overseas applicants who would be unable to attend our courses without these grants as it's important that we continue to attract participants from abroad.

And finally, the *Training Officers'* course lasts only ten weeks this year as it has been reduced in response to last year's suggestions for a slightly shorter course.

Thank you, I do hope that . . .

[pause]

tone

That is the end of Part Two.

[pause]

PART 3

Part Three
You will hear part of a radio programme in which the interviewer is talking to a woman about a speech disorder known as 'stammering'. For questions 20 to 25, choose the correct answer, A, B, C or D. You will hear the recording twice.

[pause]

tone

Interviewer: Now, a new charity is to be launched this week to help people who have a surprisingly common problem. It's called the *Association for Research into Stammering in Childhood* and with me in the studio I have Anita Andrews who's one of the founder members. Anita, can you tell me why you started this organisation?

Anita: Yes, well it's quite a triumph for me to be able to sit in front of a microphone and not talk with a d d dreadful st st stutter, (Oh, dear) and if you think listening to a stammerer or stutterer is agony, pity the poor speaker. I stammered all through my childhood until someone thought to send me to speech therapy when I was thirteen.

Interviewer: And um, how did that affect your childhood?

Anita: Well at school, in the classroom I was ignored. (Oh.) I mean the teacher would skip my turn to answer questions because it took too much time and I was always being laughed at and teased. Even today sometimes on the phone I dry up; I just can't say who I am. (Good heavens!) I longed, I used to long to act in school plays but didn't dare risk the humiliation of coming to a miserable stop with my face all twisted with the effort to speak.

Interviewer: Yes. And then, um, a nightmare came true didn't it?

Anita: Oh yes, what – with my son Joseph? (Um, yes.) Yeah, yeah. He seemed to have inherited my speech problem. In fact in order to avoid stammering he spoke so amazingly fast it was almost impossible to understand him. Of course, I whisked him off to a speech therapist but months of treatment had little effect.

Interviewer: So, how did you feel?

Anita: Well of course I was tearing out my hair. I was desperate – so we took him to the speech unit at the local hospital and they agreed to take him on a two-week intensive course in the school holiday but there was 'one condition' and that was that both parents must attend every day.

Interviewer: Goodness, that must have been difficult. Quite a commitment.

Anita: Yeah, but the therapist at the unit believes that stammering is a family affair, that the, er, behaviour of the other family members can reinforce a child's speech defect. Um, in some volatile talkative families it may be the child's only way to get attention.

Interviewer: So, did you have to go back to basics in the therapy?

Anita: Yes – yes we did. It was very strange. We had to learn to look at each other when we were talking, um, to listen properly, (yeah) er, to take turns – take turns in conversation. (Oh, right.) Well . . . we learned some not very pleasant things about ourselves really. And at the same time we learned a technique known as 'smooth speed' – making words flow together to avoid awkward and difficult sounds – very important for a stammerer.

Interviewer: And er did it help?

Anita: Oh yes – after two weeks Joseph was fluent – a different child.

Interviewer: You must be very pleased.

Anita: Well relieved really – I mean have you seen a film called 'A Fish Called Wanda'?

Interviewer: Um, oh yes, yes, yes I loved it.

Anita: Yes, well everyone laughed a great deal, but it's no joke really. One of the actors in that, Michael Palin, he based that contorted stutterer on his own father's crippling stammer. It's a film that certainly makes you think. Apparently about one per cent of the population are stammerers, and unless the condition is diagnosed and treated early it can spoil, in fact it can often completely destroy, a child's confidence. It can badly affect their academic progress, mask intelligence, and of course have a sad effect on emotional relationships.

Interviewer: Well, thank you very much for talking to us Anita and er, best of luck . . .

[pause]

tone

Now you will hear the recording again.

[The recording is repeated.]

[pause]

That is the end of Part Three.

[pause]

PART 4   *Part Four*
                You will hear five short extracts in which different people give their views
                about various means of communication. For questions 26 to 35, choose the
                correct answer, A, B or C.

                You will hear the recording twice.

                [pause]

                tone

Man: Of course, the postal service is greatly menaced by the fax machine which has
          irresistible but I think, lesser charms. There is a kind of intimacy in a letter,
          something in the fact of sealing and posting it off which doesn't exist in the fax.
          When you send a fax you never know who is going to pick it up and read it before
          passing it on to your correspondent. Also, the charm of a letter is that, if it's a good
          one, you can always re-read it. Even the letter back in response to a letter one's
          forgotten writing, carries the ghost of one's youth in it. Whereas, fax paper itself
          degenerates, in fact, and if you looked at them, I think, a year later, you'd just have
          a collection of very flimsy, almost blank pages. And that's exactly what they
          deserve to be!

Woman: I'm a bit of a phone fiend actually. I find it absolutely impossible not to answer and
          even when I go down to the end of the garden, I still carry it with me in case some
          totally unimportant person should ring. Although, as you know, telephones don't
          ring anymore, they bleep. The thing I can't abide, though, is the answering
          machine. It has such a weird effect on people's voices, the messages are certainly
          eerie. They have a kind of lifeless tenseness because, I think, they're always heavy
          with the disappointment of the person not actually having got you, so the message
          always sounds a bit sulky and demanding.

Man: Ah yes, the mobile phone is either a boon or a beast, depending on whether you've
          got one or you're surrounded by them. I am an occasional user of one myself
          actually, on the train. Now, there's a very peculiar thing about mobile phone users.
          If they're talking to a neighbour, they talk in a normal tone of voice, but if they talk
          on their mobile phone, for some reason, they shout . . . and it's impossible to read,
          to work or to take a nap, if somebody in the next part of the compartment is yelling
          down the phone, asking Ken if he can speak to Tracey and so forth. In fact you can
          mumble into the thing and still be heard quite clearly at the other end, even from a
          noisy place.

Man: As a boy, I used to spend summer holidays with a great uncle who lived on a
          remote island in Scotland. Now, he never even put in for a telephone, though he
          could have done, and I once said to him, 'But how do you talk to people? You must
          waste a lot of time,' and he replied, 'Yes, but it saves a lot of valuable time as well.
          If a man isn't worth a letter or a visit, he probably isn't worth talking to.' And then of
          course when my parents wanted to send an urgent message about last-minute
          changes to my travel plans, they had to send a telegram, which some poor soul had
          to cycle five miles with from the nearest Post Office. Terribly dramatic for me, of
          course, but my mother was mortified at causing such a fuss.

Woman: Yes, I couldn't do without a fax in my business, even if I didn't work from home, and the fax, I think, clearly has enormous advantages over the post in that everything can be completed with greater speed, but without the need to respond there and then and so get caught chatting as happens on the phone. But I sometimes dread the fax's arrival, I hate that stuttering and that sort of ah, ah, ah, which seems to go on for a very long time, and when you get there, most of the information is about how many sheets are coming or something of that kind. But when the message is eventually spewed out, it's always urgent and people get quite agitated if you don't reply immediately, even to quite complex questions.

[pause]

tone

Now you will hear the recording again.

[The recording is repeated.]

[pause]

*That is the end of Part Four. There will now be a ten minute pause to allow you to **transfer your answers to the separate answer sheet**. Be sure to follow the numbering of all the questions. The question papers and answer sheets will then be collected by your supervisor.*

Teacher, pause the tape here for ten minutes. Remind your students when they have one minute left.

That is the end of the test.

Test 3 Key

Paper 1 Reading (1 hour 15 minutes)

Part 1

1 D/G/H   2 D/G/H   3 D/G/H   4 E   5 F   6 B   7 H
8 A/H   9 A/H   10 G   11 B   12 H   13 B

Part 2

14 C   15 E   16 B   17 A   18 H   19 F   20 G

Part 3

21 B   22 D   23 C   24 C   25 A

Part 4

26 D   27 B/F   28 B/F   29 H   30 C/H   31 C/H   32 C
33 F   34 A/G/H   35 A/G/H   36 A/G/H   37 C   38 E
39 C/H/I   40 C/H/I   41 C/H/I

Paper 2 Writing (2 hours)

Part 1

Question 1

Content (points covered)
Write a letter to High Life Travel including the following points:
- accepting the invitation to work as an interpreter again
- making suggestions on how the week's programme should be improved
- making at least one suggestion on how his/her conditions of employment should be improved.

Better candidates are likely to make a judicious selection of points rather than list them all.
Letters that just criticise without accepting the job can only get a Band 2. This is not just a letter of complaint.
Better candidates will make reference to the advertisement and they will also make it clear they are speaking for others as well as themselves.

Organisation and cohesion
Letter layout is needed, with appropriate opening and closing formulae.
Addresses are not necessary.
Clear organisation. Better candidates are likely to present the three parts of the letter making good use of paragraphing.

128

Range
Language of criticism and suggestion.
Better candidates may show the ability to display tact when criticising and when asking for improved conditions.

Register
Consistently formal.

Target reader
Would understand all the points being made without being offended by the criticisms i.e. would not want to withdraw the job offer.

Part 2

Question 2

Content (points covered)
Candidates must write an article for the newsletter.
There must be some reference to:
• problems experienced
• benefits gained
when using English for work or study.

Organisation and cohesion
Clear organisation of main points with appropriate use of paragraphs.

Range
Vocabulary and structures appropriate for describing personal experience, problems and benefits.

Register
Consistently formal, neutral or semi-formal.

Target reader
Would be informed and would consider including the article in the newsletter.

Question 3

Content (points covered)
The candidate must write the text for a leaflet describing some items of interest from the candidate's country.
The leaflet should:
• describe the items (these could be all of one type e.g. a collection of paintings)
• refer to the history of the items
• explain the importance of the items.
NB It is sufficient for a Band 3 to mention the importance of the items in universal terms.
The leaflet could be to attract visitors to the exhibition or it could be for those who have already turned up.

Organisation and cohesion
Clear layout appropriate to a publicity leaflet.

Range
Language of description appropriate to the items and their significance.

Register
Consistently neutral, formal or possibly informal.

Target reader
Would be well informed.

Question 4

Content (points covered)
The candidate must write an article for an international English language magazine. The article must discuss the changing role of women in the candidate's country, focusing on at least one of the following areas:
- the workplace and careers
- marriage and relationships
- housework
- politics
- education.

NB For a Band 3 it is not necessary to make direct reference to the situation in the past as long as it is implicit that there have been changes.
It may also be possible to argue that nothing has changed.
It should be evident that the candidate is referring to a particular country rather than talking about the changing role of women in general.

Organisation and cohesion
Clear organisation with appropriate use of paragraphs.

Range
Language describing change. Vocabulary and structure relating to the aspect of society under discussion.

Register
Consistently neutral or formal.

Target reader
Would be informed.

Question 5

Content (points covered)
The candidate must write a character reference for someone s/he has known for a long time. This must include the following points:
- how long s/he has known the person
- her/his relationship with the candidate
- the strengths of the candidate.

NB Reasons for supporting the candidate may be implicit in the second and third points above.
Better candidates are likely to introduce a balance between strengths and weaknesses and link these specifically to children.

Organisation and cohesion
Clear layout with suitable paragraphing. Letter format acceptable.
Appropriate introduction and conclusion.

Range
Language of description and recommendation appropriate to the person.

Register
Consistently formal or neutral.

Target reader
Would be informed and would give consideration to the application.

Paper 3 English in Use (1 hour 30 minutes)

(1 mark for each correct answer)

Part 1

1 A (field)   2 C (occupation)   3 B (given)   4 A (encounter)
5 D (established)   6 C (demand)   7 C (specimen)   8 A (eager)
9 A (substantial)   10 D (suitable)   11 D (result)   12 B (probably)
13 B (reject)   14 A (impressed)   15 C (similar)

Part 2

16 more   17 in/with   18 rather   19 from
20 because/as/since/for   21 at   22 one   23 being
24 the/so/its   25 there   26 from/before   27 about/over   28 are
29 for   30 where

Part 3

31 America, Europe   32 ✓   33 decorate   34 particular, took
35 precious   36 improvement   37 as 'paste'   38 diamonds   39 ✓
40 thousands   41 French   42 imitation   43 used to
44 completely   45 ✓   46 affordable

Part 4

47 varieties   48 impossible   49 enthusiastic   50 preference
51 perfection   52 briefly   53 essential

54 extraordinary   55 adventurous   56 activities   57 selection
58 endless   59 spacious   60 affordable   61 especially

Part 5

62 qualification in/certificate in/diploma in
63 manner/voice
64 quite well/reasonably well/fairly well/satisfactorily/well enough
65 driving licence
66 keen on/interested in/fond of
67 with style/stylishly/well
68 (good/keen/nice) sense
69 confident/relaxed/comfortable
70 suited to/suited for/suitable for/qualified for/appropriate for
71 be improved/improve/be better
72 (very) prompt/punctual/on time
73 offers/an offer/any offer/the offer
74 current/present//responsibilities/duties

Part 6

75 F   76 H   77 D   78 G   79 A   80 C

Paper 4 Listening (45 minutes)

Part 1

1 1000   2 1 year   3 8 years   4 £10–£15   5 200 m(illion)
6 $3\frac{1}{2}$ m(illion)   7 local electrical supplier   8 80% *or* £30

Part 2

9 stable(s)/farmyard   10 reception (room)   11 office(s)
12 slaves' quarters/building/barracks/rooms/storeroom for slaves
13 library   14 bathroom/bath-house
15 women's quarters/building/barracks/rooms
16 kitchen   17 hospital   18 food store

Part 3

19 D   20 D   21 C   22 D   23 A

Part 4

24 H   25 F   26 A   27 E   28 C
29 E   30 A   31 D   32 F   33 B

Transcript

This is the Cambridge Certificate in Advanced English Listening Test. Test Three.

This paper requires you to listen to a selection of recorded material and answer the accompanying questions.

*There are four parts to the test, **One, Two, Three** and **Four**. You will hear Part Two **once** only. All the other parts of the test will be heard twice.*

There will be a pause before each part to allow you to look through the questions, and other pauses to let you think about your answers. At the end of every pause you will hear this sound.

tone

*You should write your answers on the **question** paper. You will have **ten** minutes at the end to **transfer your answers to the separate answer sheet**.*

The tape will now be stopped. You must ask any questions now as you will not be allowed to speak during the test.

[pause]

PART 1

Now open your question paper and look at Part One.

[pause]

Part One
You will hear a recording of an interview with Edward Munns, a representative from the Lighting Industry Federation. He is talking about a new type of environmentally-friendly lightbulb. For questions 1 to 8, complete the information. You will hear the recording twice.

[pause]

tone

Presenter: Environmentally-friendly lightbulbs have been around for the last ten years but are not as widely used as you might expect. They may save electricity and last many years longer, but the first versions weren't exactly stylish; and they were hardly *light* bulbs either, they were heavy bulbs that could pull your wiring out of the ceiling. The latest developments though are much improved as Edward Munns from the Lighting Industry Federation explains.

Edward Munns: The general movement is towards products which are lighter in weight, and smaller, and give better light. They come in all shapes and sizes so there are some very close in shape to the traditional standard lightbulbs that you can buy. On average the standard or ordinary lightbulb lasts a thousand hours; if you have it on for just under three hours a day, it'll last a year. These new ones will last eight times as long, so they could last eight years. Now as to price: well, they cost anything from £10 to £15, depending on the wattage – admittedly much more than a standard lightbulb. At present, however, very few have been sold. In the UK, well, I would guess that it's something like three and a half million which may sound a lot, but when you think over 200 million of the standard type are sold, well, you can see it's very, very small. But once the volumes build up, well who knows?
 There is a problem in getting shops like supermarkets to stock them, though,

133

because of the high capital cost. But we're hoping to persuade them this winter to start for all sorts of reasons. But if you have problems, one of the easiest ways to get hold of them is to contact your local electrical supplier. He'll almost certainly have them in stock. And you'll get a financial return in a reasonable amount of time if you put them in the places where they're used a lot. Over the life of one of these lamps, over the life of 8,000 hours, you could save as much as £30, or 80% of your normal electricity cost. I have them downstairs in my house, because I have teenage children who are incapable of switching the lights off, and so when I come down in the morning and find the house absolutely ablaze with light, at least I can comfort myself with the thought that it's only costing me a fifth of what it would otherwise cost.

[pause]

tone

Now you will hear the recording again.

[The recording is repeated.]

[pause]

That is the end of Part One.

[pause]

PART 2

Part Two
Look at the plan of Bankeira, an archaeological site. You will hear a tour guide conducting a party of visitors around the site. For questions 9 to 18, fill in the name of each building in the appropriate space. Listen very carefully as you will hear the recording ONCE only.

[pause]

tone

Guide: Ladies and gentlemen, welcome to Bankeira. You have heard in the museum something of the civilisation which is presumed to have been responsible for these buildings in front of us. Now, it's my pleasure to conduct you round the site itself. If you'd like to follow me? Now, if we follow the track here between these two walls . . . you can probably distinguish a contrast in style, in spite of the weathering. This is, we believe, an indication of the different functions of the two buildings. The first, on our right here, is quite roughly-dressed stone, and from other evidence we are fairly certain this was accommodation for animals, probably known as 'the farmyard', and we think these particular stables here would have been for the saddle horses.

On our left, the large chamber of very finely-dressed stone was certainly the reception room, where visitors would have been entertained. It's conveniently located here at the front of the site, away from more private and domestic offices. There are remnants of decorative work visible inside; you probably saw pictures of it in the museum. Unfortunately the fabric is not safe enough for us to go in now.

Now if we walk on, towards the third building, behind these most public areas . . .

we come to what was evidently a suite of small rooms, the use of which puzzled our experts for a long time, until a description of a similar site was found in a poem of about this date, which made it clear that the master and his assistants conducted the business of the estate here, so in fact this was the office where the accounts were paid and so on. Unfortunately, (*laugh*) no coins have been found as yet! If you look over to the right, there is a large L-shaped area, which I'm sorry to say, would have been regarded by the master as the storeroom for a part of his property. Over a hundred slaves lived here, and they would all have been squashed into that space – doesn't seem so big for a hundred people does it? The reason it's not so well-preserved is because less stone and more wood was used in its construction – even compared to where the horses were kept, I'm afraid.

Over on the left, the long building beyond the reception room is where the master could relax among his books, with learned and cultured friends. There were no traces of any of the fine volumes left when we came to excavate, of course, but similar libraries elsewhere have been described in detail. Now, the little square building next to it, I wonder if anyone could hazard a guess? I think it's an indication of the extremely pleasant lifestyle of the wealthy residents here.

You see the stone channels in the ground? They served to carry hot water for the bath in here, so the master could lie in his tub here in the bath-house and listen to music provided by musicians in the library! And, er, you see the building behind the bathroom? That was the women's quarters, where the wife and daughters lived. Of course, they never appeared in public, but it seems that they were quite free, and exercised considerable influence within the household itself.

Beyond the bathroom, the larger building was the kitchen, for the family's meals only of course, the slaves had to make do as best they could in their wooden barracks, and between the kitchen and the back end of the slave quarters was the hospital building. They had no idea of keeping the sick away from other people, or from food preparation areas! The little building behind the kitchen where the floor is so far below ground level was designed to keep the food stored there at an even temperature.

Now, if you'd like to follow me up the small hill, we can get an excellent impression of the site as a whole . . .

[pause]

tone

That is the end of Part Two.

[pause]

PART 3

Part Three
You will hear part of a radio interview with the actress Susan Davenant who is starring in a successful TV series called 'The Falling Leaves'. For questions 19 to 23, choose the correct answers from A, B, C or D. You will hear the recording twice.

[pause]

tone

Barry: We're very pleased to have with us this afternoon the star of the highly successful current TV series, 'The Falling Leaves', Susan Davenant. Susan, hello and welcome.

Susan: Hello Barry. Lovely to be here.

Barry: Was it a pleasure making the series?

Susan: Well, Barry, working on things like this is hard work and it's really hard if things aren't going right – then you end up only doing it for the money. But fortunately we gelled really well and some of us had worked together before, so we knew each other, (uh-huh) not that that is necessarily a recipe for success, but in the event there was some kind of rare electricity between us.

Barry: I think that comes across. Any bad moments?

Susan: Oh, one or two, yes. I remember one day, I just couldn't get my lines right, and we did this scene over and over again, must have been twenty times, and everybody was beginning to stop smiling and get fed up with me, you know, you could tell by the way their smiles were ever closer to scowls as they glanced at me! And I got so frustrated with myself. I stormed off the set – really! (*Laugh*) The director had to come and calm me down. Eventually, I went back on the set, and got it right first time. Everyone clapped in mock admiration, and we all laughed about it.

Barry: (*Laugh*) Lovely. Now, Susan, if I may say so, in the series you look considerably plumper than you actually are.

Susan: (*Laugh*) Oh, yes. Well, I'm naturally quite slim, and this was a problem. I didn't look credible, slim. In fact what they did was they padded me out a bit to look the part.

Barry: Which is a buxom farmer's wife, isn't it?

Susan: That's right. Somehow you couldn't imagine a character like that without an ample figure, shall we say? In fact, I did try to gain weight for the part, because I like to prepare myself physically as well as mentally.

Barry: So you put on a few pounds?

Susan: Uh-huh, but not enough to look convincing enough for the director. So they added bits here and there.

Barry: Yes, I was just going to say . . .

Susan: Oh but, but Barry, just let me say one advantage has turned out to be that I don't always have the problem of being recognised everywhere I go.

Barry: In fact, I was going to ask you, do you find it embarrassing or irritating, people coming up to you?

Susan: Oh, no, no. But I do understand. I mean, they come up to you because they want to tell people they've spoken to someone famous. It's a kind of occupational hazard.

Barry: Yes. Susan, after this series, what's next?

Susan: Well, I know that many actors and actresses have a great success and then have never been heard of again. But I hope that I'm sufficiently versatile not to end up stereotyped, and to be offered more parts. I'm already working on another TV series . . .

Barry: Oh?

Susan: . . . which should be on your screens this autumn! Quite different, a thriller set in the forties in London. Plus, my first love is the theatre, and I'm going to do some Shakespeare next year, as well as some film work.

Barry: Um. I hear talk of a sequel to 'The Falling Leaves' . . .

Susan: That's right. I hope that comes off.

Barry: Quite a variety then? (Um.) Where do your true ambitions lie, then?

Susan: I enjoy what I'm doing, of course. But I'd say that what I'd really like to be thought of as, is a good classical actress. (Ah.) I've yet to do any of the great Shakespeare roles, but I would always choose the stage over the screen, there's nothing to compare with live performance.

Barry: So, what are you doing next . . .

[pause]

tone

Now you will hear the recording again.

[The recording is repeated.]

[pause]

That is the end of Part Three.

[pause]

PART 4   *Part Four*
You will hear five short extracts, in which various people are talking about food. Task One. For questions 24 to 28, match the extracts as you hear them with the people listed A to H. Task Two. For questions 29 to 33, match the extracts as you hear them with each speaker's intention listed A to H.

You will hear the recording twice.

[pause]

tone

Man: No need to say anything really is there? The silence tells it all. (*Laugh*) I don't know how you do it, François – absolutely terrific. Who, who would've thought it with such peculiar ingredients (*laugh*) – I'm glad you didn't let us know 'til after we'd finished. I'd never have said yes to the invitation if you'd told us what we were in for but, er, I take my hat off to you. Next time you must, er, come round to us – that's two we owe you.

Woman: You need the freshest apples mind. You cut them up and put in a few sultanas – they've got some good ones down at the market, they sell them loose. You could always pop in and borrow some from me if you haven't the time to get out. Then you add in the lemon juice – watch out there's no pips in it, and sprinkle on a bit more of the sugar. Leave it to stand for a good bit I should . . .

Woman: The fish provides a rich source of protein and this is balanced by the fats in the sauce – the mixture of dairy products and flour. Of course, fibre could be provided by say, er brown bread and more bulk if necessary by potatoes or rice, which also provide starch, which is . . .

Man: You can't just eat the potatoes on their own, there's not enough goodness in them. You've got to eat some vegetables so you get things like iron and vitamins. And look, just that little bit of fish has all the protein you need to keep you going all day. It's not as if you're fat or anything . . . now come on, eat up . . .

Chef: You place the bowl in the hot water and then stir the butter into the mixture. You have to keep adding it slowly, that's absolutely vital, otherwise you've got real problems because as the meals come through you've got to serve it and then keep adding so the consistency and the proportions stay the same. Take your eyes off it for a minute and you've lost the whole batch . . .

[pause]

tone

Now you will hear the recording again.

[The recording is repeated.]

[pause]

*That is the end of Part Four. There will now be a ten minute pause to allow you to **transfer your answers to the separate answer sheet**. Be sure to follow the numbering of all the questions. The question papers and answer sheets will then be collected by your supervisor.*

Teacher, pause the tape here for ten minutes. Remind your students when they have one minute left.

That is the end of the test.

Test 4 Key

Paper 1 Reading (1 hour 15 minutes)

Part 1

1 A   2 B   3 E   4 D   5 A   6 C   7 A/B   8 A/B
9 B   10 D   11 A   12 D   13 B   14 B/C   15 B/C
16 B   17 A

Part 2

18 B   19 E   20 D   21 H   22 A   23 G   24 C

Part 3

25 C   26 D   27 B   28 D   29 D

Part 4

30 G   31 F   32 A   33 H   34 C   35 A   36 E/F
37 E/F   38 C/G   39 C/G   40 C   41 F

Paper 2 Writing (2 hours)

Part 1

Question 1

Content (points covered)
A report with at least a balanced reference to (a) problems experienced and (b) benefits gained from the job. Best candidates will make a judicious selection of points rather than list them all. Reports that just criticise or praise or make no reference to other team leaders' views can only get a Band 2. There must be a balance.

Organisation and cohesion
It is a report, *not* a letter. Clear presentation of the various points either in paragraphs or with sub-headings. A purposeful opening and a brief conclusion. Cohesive connection of description of the camp experience.

Range
Competent use of both factual language and the language of personal opinion and reporting other views. Ability to summarise, describing clearly the problems and benefits.

Register
Neutral. Could be fairly informal but should be consistent with some enthusiasm evident.

Target reader
Potential new team leaders would be informed and interested.

Part 2

Question 2
Content (points covered)
Could be leaflet to attract visitors to the town or it could be for those who have already turned up. Description of places to visit/things to do, within the time available (morning or afternoon); they could be all in one category e.g. parks, museums or only a single attraction but should include reasons why. Some information about location, entry times, charges etc.

Organisation and cohesion
Clear layout appropriate to a publicity leaflet – title/paragraphs/sub-headings. (Artistic ability not assessed!)

Range
Language describing particular places. Vocabulary/structures to explain significance/interest of places. Language of suggestion, recommendations. Not necessarily complex structures.

Register
Neutral/formal. (Candidates might choose to write about places aimed at children and then register might be more informal.)

Target reader
Would be interested enough to visit the places described and would be informed.

Question 3
Content (points covered)
Letter describing the musical event with a clear reference/description of why it did/did not come up to expectations. Information about the venue/charge, focusing on the strengths or weaknesses of the concert. (Could be performance or other related matter.) Implicit/explicit reference to friend's taste in music. Clear statement of the festival/concert being referred to – performer and venue.

Organisation and cohesion
Clear presentation in letter format without too much preamble – introduction, description, conclusion/appropriate ending with paragraphs. Address not necessary.

Range
Language of description and personal opinion. Vocabulary relating to music/concert and sharing views. Range of past tenses.

Register
Informal, even chatty – must be consistent.

Target reader
Would be interested and informed and understand why it did/did not come up to expectations.

Question 4

Content (points covered)
Article addressed to college students, so at least some reference to more than one article/possession which a student would have (e.g. computer, bike, books, camera etc.). Focus on recommendations/suggestions (not personal horror stories).

Organisation and cohesion
It is an article and so there should be an attempt to engage readers from the beginning (a prize is offered). Clear layout, possibly with sub-headings, not a list of instructions.

Range
Vocabulary and structures appropriate for suggestion – clear explanation of what one can do to protect possessions. Language describing security measures.

Register
Could be formal (like police brochure) or fairly informal but it must be consistent.

Target reader
Would be informed, made aware of possible dangers in order to take appropriate precautions.

Question 5

Content (points covered)
Description of specific behaviour in business situations in own country, which should be stated. (Inappropriate to dwell exclusively on anecdotal experiences, especially negative ones. Factual approach needed, not personal experience.)

Organisation and cohesion
Guide format, *not* letter. Clear introduction explaining purpose of guide. Obvious paragraphs/sub-headings for three basic aspects.

Range
Ability to display tact when describing own/other country and its habits. Vocabulary relating to dress/behaviour.

Register
Formal/neutral.

Target reader
Would understand all the points being made and feel well prepared to cope in a business situation.

Paper 3 English in Use (1 hour 30 minutes)

(1 mark for each correct answer)

Part 1

1 C (powerless)   2 A (nature)   3 B (the public)   4 B (thrive)
5 C (committed)   6 A (peak)   7 D (risk)   8 A (varies)
9 C (reliance)   10 D (key)   11 B (bother)   12 A (force)
13 C (tackling)   14 D (coping)   15 A (quality)

Part 2

16 with   17 a/their/some   18 would   19 what   20 people
21 still/also   22 of   23 because   24 on/upon   25 the
26 made   27 that/which   28 can/will/should/must/could/shall
29 in/during/through   30 for

Part 3

31 vice'.   32 thousands   33 pairs   34 tramps and   35 queued
36 ✓   37 doorways   38 ✓   39 Canada   40 themselves
41 ex-criminal   42 ✓   43 achievement   44 which   45 residents
46 families

Part 4

47 novelists   48 impressive   49 humorous   50 pleasure
51 thoughtful   52 collection   53 disappointment
54 brilliance   55 prominently   56 architecture   57 relationship
58 astronomer   59 observation(s)   60 presence   61 invisible

Part 5

62 pleased/satisfied/happy/impressed/content   63 better planned
64 aimed too   65 went up   66 asked to/expected to/supposed to
67 too long   68 slang/informal language   69 wrong word
70 approved   71 (photo)copied   72 mistakes/typos
73 ruined/spoiled   74 gave/handed/sent

Part 6

75 D   76 I   77 A   78 F   79 G   80 B

Paper 4 Listening (45 minutes)

Part 1

1 rose/increased   2 five   3 fell/declined   4 two or three/two to three
5 wholemeal/untreated/different   6 healthier/healthy/good for you

7 travel/travelling/holidays abroad/foreign travel *or* foreign food/foreign/ethnic
restaurant
8 foreign food/foreign/ethnic restaurants *or* travel/travelling/holidays abroad/
foreign travel
9 olives *or* seeds   10 seeds *or* olives

Part 2

11 Room 6   12 Communication(s)   13 Room 5   14 Memorial Hall
15 Bishop's Hall One   16 self-service restaurant   17 Bishop's Hall Two
18 Room 5   19 Assembly Hall   20 Abbey Room   21 7.30

Part 3

22 D   23 C   24 A   25 A   26 A   27 B   28 D

Part 4

29 A   30 B   31 B   32 C   33 B
34 C   35 B   36 B   37 A   38 B

Transcript *This is the Cambridge Certificate in Advanced English Listening Test. Test Four.*

This paper requires you to listen to a selection of recorded material and answer the accompanying questions.

*There are four parts to the test, **One, Two, Three** and **Four**. You will hear Part Two **once** only. All the other parts of the test will be heard twice.*

There will be a pause before each part to allow you to look through the questions, and other pauses to let you think about your answers. At the end of every pause you will hear this sound.

tone

*You should write your answers on the **question** paper. You will have **ten** minutes at the end to **transfer your answers to the separate answer sheet**.*

The tape will now be stopped. You must ask any questions now as you will not be allowed to speak during the test.

[pause]

PART 1   *Now open your question paper and look at Part One.*

[pause]

Part One
You will hear part of a radio programme on food. Janet, a journalist who specialises in cookery, is giving a talk about bread. For questions 1 to 10, complete the notes. You will hear the recording twice.

[pause]

tone

Janet: Bread. Are you eating more of it or less than you used to? The amount of bread being eaten, according to the National Federation of Master Bakers, is increasing. Last year we ate about five per cent more bread than the year before, and this reversed what had been a constant decline of two or three per cent a year for the previous ten years or so. However, in that ten years, the kind of bread being eaten changed remarkably. I suppose the most obvious change is that an increasing number of people are now opting for brown bread as opposed to white, and this brown bread itself is tending to be made from different flour than it used to be. Whereas in the past, say twenty or twenty-five years ago, most people ate white bread made with bleached white flour or brown bread, both with most of the fibre taken out, now people are more and more going for brown wholemeal bread, that is, bread made with untreated wheat flour, and they seem to be happy to pay a higher price for it. This tendency mirrors current beliefs about health, of course, principally that fibre is good for you.

But that isn't all. There's been an increase in the variety of bread available as well, by which I mean recipes and types of loaf. Twenty years ago, the average baker baked about three sorts of loaf in this country. But things are changing. Clearly, this is partly the result of travelling.

Ordinary people now more often go abroad for their holidays than stay in Britain, and whilst abroad they pick up a taste for different foods, bread among them. What's more, at home there is an increasing tendency in Britain to eat in so-called 'foreign restaurants', such as Greek, Italian or Spanish, where customers are offered different bread, which they then ask for at the baker's when they're out shopping. It's surprising how much restaurants are responsible for changing people's taste in food, and bread is no exception.

The result of this has been an explosion in the kinds of bread available. So, what might you find at an adventurous baker's or supermarket near you? Rye breads, breads made of wheat and rye flour blends, loaves with seed sprinkled all over them or baked in, and now, the latest thing is bread with olives in, black or green, and then there's soft grain bread, where the whole wheat-grain is softened by a new process, and mixed with flour. If you haven't begun to already, I do advise you to experiment and try these really appetising varieties of bread. . . .

[pause]

tone

Now you will hear the recording again.

[The recording is repeated.]

[pause]

That is the end of Part One.

[pause]

PART 2   *Part Two*
You will hear an introduction to a course in Business Management Today. For questions 11 to 21, complete the information. Listen very carefully as you will hear the recording ONCE only.

[pause]

tone

Man: Good morning and welcome to our course on 'Business Management Today'. I hope you've all registered and obtained your name badges and information packs. I would like to point out some additional information and changes to the agenda you will find in your packs. The four seminar workshops are now as follows:

Room Six – 'Marketing'.

Bishop's Hall One – 'Communications', which replaces 'Taxation'.

Bishop's Hall Two – 'Strategic Planning', which now includes small businesses, as well as large companies.

Room Five – 'Human Resources'.

I'll just run through that again. 'Marketing' is in Room Six. In Bishop's Hall One we have a change to the original programme, and 'Taxation' has been replaced by 'Communications'. 'Strategic Planning' in Bishop's Hall Two now includes small businesses, and Room Five is 'Human Resources'.

We will stay in the Convocation Hall for the first morning session, which runs from nine-thirty till eleven o'clock, when we shall all meet up in the Memorial Hall for coffee and biscuits.

The eleven-thirty session will be held in Bishop's Hall One.

A buffet lunch will be held in the self-service restaurant from one to two. We are hoping that this system will prove quicker than waitress service, and ensure a prompt start to the afternoon session which begins in Bishop's Hall Two at two o'clock and runs to three-thirty. Please note, however, that we shall be in Room Five for the four to five-thirty session.

Tea and biscuits will be brought to you between three-thirty to four o'clock.

At five-thirty, we invite you all to the Assembly Hall for an hour's general forum. There will be time for questions based on the day's sessions. This session in the Assembly Hall is intended to give you an opportunity to clarify any problem areas which may have arisen during the day and to ask any questions you may have. There will be a general exhibition of books and resource materials in the Abbey Room, which will be open for the whole day. Anyone interested in purchasing any of these materials will be able to order them at the various stands.

Please feel free to visit the Abbey Room at any time during the day up until the Centre closes at seven-thirty pm.

May I draw your attention to the fact that notes accompanying the seminars will be provided by the speakers. It is therefore not necessary . . .

[pause]

tone

That is the end of Part Two.

[pause]

PART 3   *Part Three*
You will hear part of a radio programme for university students. For questions 22 to 28, choose the correct answer A, B, C or D.

You will hear the recording twice.

[pause]

tone

Presenter:	And now it's time for our weekly 'In the Hot Seat' spot, in which we talk to university students about their aims, hopes and experiences. This week, our reporter Sandra Guff went to Lowland University, where she spoke to Tony Wall, a Media Studies student who is about to finish his course.
Sandra:	Well, Tony, welcome to the Hot Seat. First of all I want to ask you why you chose your course.
Tony:	Well, when I started thinking about going to university, I wanted to do something that would interest me – I wasn't so concerned about what it might lead to. I didn't have anything specific in mind and a couple of my teachers came up with this idea – they thought it was the sort of thing that might suit me. My parents had wanted me to follow in their footsteps I think – they've got their own business – but they came round to the idea eventually.
Sandra:	Now if you had the choice, what would be your ideal job?
Tony:	Ideally, I'd like to be a TV presenter. I mean, you have to put up with a lot of people going on and on about their latest book or film or whatever and you have to like being approached by people in supermarkets for your autograph – I'm probably not the ideal person for all that – but it always looks to me like there's nothing to it. You ask a few silly questions and you get a few silly answers.
Sandra:	Do you think you could get that job?
Tony:	I doubt it. It's a ruthless business and there are so many people trying to do it that very few succeed, and I shouldn't think I'd be one of them. I mean, you can be as determined as you like and you can have loads of talent but in the end it's all about luck. I could certainly do it, but I'll probably have to settle for being a journalist on a paper.
Sandra:	Would you consider working abroad?
Tony:	No, no, I don't think so. I mean, I'm not great at languages and it would probably be hard for me to get a media job abroad, but that's not really it. I wouldn't mind the challenge of getting used to another way of life but to be honest I'd be lost without stuff like the football and my friends over here.
Sandra:	How do you rate your course?
Tony:	Well, the teachers have been great and I feel that I've got a lot out of what they've taught me. I was always pretty good at organising myself with regard to work but what they've given me is a thorough grounding in the theory – and more importantly how to apply it. I can't say it's been all that thrilling but I think all in all it's been worth doing.
Sandra:	What do you think your future earnings will be like?
Tony:	Yes that's something I've just started to think about. It never mattered to me before but it sort of does now. Pay in journalism isn't usually all that good for most people and that's just something you have to accept, but I reckon that maybe I can do quite well for myself after a while.
Sandra:	What would you most like to be doing in ten years' time?
Tony:	Well of course a lot of journalists are frustrated novelists and I'm no different, but I doubt whether I'll ever get round to doing that. I suppose I wouldn't mind editing a paper or even running my own magazine but somehow I can't see that happening. I think that by then the best I can hope for is that I'm doing a regular 'opinion piece' – commenting on recent events, something like that.
Sandra:	When you leave university, what will you miss most about being a student?
Tony:	Good question. I suppose the friends I've made have been a big part of this period in my life, but I expect I'll keep in touch with them. We've had some pretty wild

parties, I can tell you, but you can't go on forever doing that, can you? Of course my working hours will be more regular than I've been used to but that's probably not such a bad thing. I think it'll be not having the sheer freedom I've had that I'll find hardest to adjust to.

Sandra: And what will you miss least?

Tony: What springs to mind is the way everyone goes on about everyone else behind their backs – that gets on my nerves. Also, I've lived in some pretty terrible places over the last few years, although funnily enough, now that's over I feel a sort of peculiar affection for them. The work's been a problem sometimes and some of the lectures have been a terrible bore but you soon forget about that sort of thing, don't you?

Sandra: Thanks, Tony, for being 'In the Hot Seat' this week, and all the best for the future.

Tony: My pleasure.

[pause]

tone

Now you will hear the recording again.

[The recording is repeated.]

[pause]

That is the end of Part Three.

[pause]

PART 4

Part Four
You will hear five short extracts, in which different people say what they attribute their success to. For questions 29 to 38, choose the correct answer A, B or C.

You will hear the recording twice.

[pause]

tone

Man: After I left school I began to realise doing unskilled work wasn't going to get me far, and one day I just happened to be reading the paper and I saw an advertisement for evening classes in this subject which I had thought about, you know, casually. And I enrolled, really took to it, and worked and worked and worked, every evening for six years. Certainly it had a disturbing effect on my social and home life, though my parents were wonderful. It's about self-respect and proving yourself – that's what I got out of it, and nobody suffered, except me for a bit!

Man: There was music in the family and when I started to show an interest, my parents encouraged it. I think practice is important, technique matters. I used to practise a lot when I was younger, but I don't overdo it now. No amount of practice makes up for natural aptitude, I'm afraid. That's not arrogance. It's true, and I'm thankful for being gifted. Incidentally, you say I've become a household name, which is very nice, of course, but what matters is, er, I can – if I may say so – enrich other people's lives, artistically, now I'm in a position to finance the studies of needy talented people. I had to struggle so I understand the position they're in.

Woman: I've achieved just what I wanted to, once I realised what it was. My parents were always on at me to succeed at school, particularly my father, and I rebelled, in fact I did just the opposite of what they wanted, and left with a few pretty worthless exams. I was aimless, to tell the truth, but I got talking to a girl I met in a disco one evening and she was a dental nurse and got me interested in it as a career. You see, I'd been quite good at Biology and things like that at school, which was relevant. So I was able to train, and now I work for this person who really motivates you and gets you involved, with lots to do – you know – and not just hanging around in the background. For instance, she introduces me to patients, almost like an equal. I've really landed on my feet. I couldn't ask for more.

Man: I'd been running a family business – we were bakers – and that's what I'd expected to be doing for ever, really, until one day, through no fault of my own, the business failed. I was devastated, of course. Then I pulled myself together. I remembered a childhood ambition, to be a lawyer. So despite my age, I decided to try it. I went round every law firm in this town, and it's a big town – refusal after refusal. But I don't give up easily and I went on until I found a firm that would agree to take me on as a trainee. They were very supportive, and respected maturity – they didn't think I was too old – nor did I! – that was the point, and they were unusual in that. Well, to cut a long story short they offered me a partnership in the firm after a few years, and I've never looked back.

Woman: When I got a bit too old for sailing, I found that my being well-known meant that I got plenty of offers of work, which was good – ranging from people asking me to manage teams and organise whole events to writing books. But what I settled on was TV – commentating on sports events, which is really satisfying, because I get assignments all over the globe. And I still use the same approach as I've always done: be thorough; think ahead. I wouldn't have been so successful if I hadn't. It's as simple as that. I never leave anything to chance or assume I'm going to have good luck; no, never plan for good luck. I didn't sail around the world alone twice assuming I'd have good weather on the difficult bits.

[pause]

tone

Now you will hear the recording again.

[The recording is repeated.]

[pause]

*That is the end of Part Four. There will now be a ten minute pause to allow you to **transfer your answers to the separate answer sheet**. Be sure to follow the numbering of all the questions. The question papers and answer sheets will then be collected by your supervisor.*

Teacher, pause the tape here for ten minutes. Remind your students when they have one minute left.

That is the end of the test.

UNIVERSITY *of* CAMBRIDGE
Local Examinations Syndicate

SAMPLE

Candidate Name
If not already printed, write name
in CAPITALS and complete the
Candidate No. grid (in pencil).

Candidate's signature

Examination Title

Centre

Supervisor:

☒ If the candidate is ABSENT or has WITHDRAWN shade here ▭

Centre No.

Candidate No.

**Examination
Details**

0	0	0	0
1	1	1	1
2	2	2	2
3	3	3	3
4	4	4	4
5	5	5	5
6	6	6	6
7	7	7	7
8	8	8	8
9	9	9	9

Multiple-choice Answer Sheet

Use a pencil   Mark one letter for each question.

For example:

If you think C is the right answer to the
question, mark your answer sheet like this:

Change your answer
like this:

1	A B C D E F G H I
2	A B C D E F G H I
3	A B C D E F G H I
4	A B C D E F G H I
5	A B C D E F G H I
6	A B C D E F G H I
7	A B C D E F G H I
8	A B C D E F G H I
9	A B C D E F G H I
10	A B C D E F G H I
11	A B C D E F G H I
12	A B C D E F G H I
13	A B C D E F G H I
14	A B C D E F G H I
15	A B C D E F G H I
16	A B C D E F G H I
17	A B C D E F G H I
18	A B C D E F G H I
19	A B C D E F G H I
20	A B C D E F G H I

21	A B C D E F G H I
22	A B C D E F G H I
23	A B C D E F G H I
24	A B C D E F G H I
25	A B C D E F G H I
26	A B C D E F G H I
27	A B C D E F G H I
28	A B C D E F G H I
29	A B C D E F G H I
30	A B C D E F G H I
31	A B C D E F G H I
32	A B C D E F G H I
33	A B C D E F G H I
34	A B C D E F G H I
35	A B C D E F G H I
36	A B C D E F G H I
37	A B C D E F G H I
38	A B C D E F G H I
39	A B C D E F G H I
40	A B C D E F G H I

41	A B C D E F G H I
42	A B C D E F G H I
43	A B C D E F G H I
44	A B C D E F G H I
45	A B C D E F G H I
46	A B C D E F G H I
47	A B C D E F G H I
48	A B C D E F G H I
49	A B C D E F G H I
50	A B C D E F G H I
51	A B C D E F G H I
52	A B C D E F G H I
53	A B C D E F G H I
54	A B C D E F G H I
55	A B C D E F G H I
56	A B C D E F G H I
57	A B C D E F G H I
58	A B C D E F G H I
59	A B C D E F G H I
60	A B C D E F G H I

UNIVERSITY *of* CAMBRIDGE
Local Examinations Syndicate

SAMPLE

Candidate Name
If not already printed, write name
in CAPITALS and complete the
Candidate No. grid (in pencil).

Candidate's signature

- -

Examination Title

Centre

Supervisor:

☒ If the candidate is ABSENT or has WITHDRAWN shade here ⊏⊐

Centre No.

Candidate No.

Examination Details

0	0	0	0
1	1	1	1
2	2	2	2
3	3	3	3
4	4	4	4
5	5	5	5
6	6	6	6
7	7	7	7
8	8	8	8
9	9	9	9

—
—
—
—

Candidate Answer Sheet

Use a pencil

For **Parts 1** and **6:**
Mark ONE letter for each question.
For example, if you think **B** is the
right answer to the question,
mark your answer sheet like this:

0 A B̲ C̲ D̲

For **Parts 2, 3, 4** and **5:**
Write your answers in the spaces
next to the numbers like this:

0 *example*

Part 1				
1	A	B	C	D
2	A	B	C	D
3	A	B	C	D
4	A	B	C	D
5	A	B	C	D
6	A	B	C	D
7	A	B	C	D
8	A	B	C	D
9	A	B	C	D
10	A	B	C	D
11	A	B	C	D
12	A	B	C	D
13	A	B	C	D
14	A	B	C	D
15	A	B	C	D

Part 2 — Do not write here

16		⊏ 16 ⊐
17		⊏ 17 ⊐
18		⊏ 18 ⊐
19		⊏ 19 ⊐
20		⊏ 20 ⊐
21		⊏ 21 ⊐
22		⊏ 22 ⊐
23		⊏ 23 ⊐
24		⊏ 24 ⊐
25		⊏ 25 ⊐
26		⊏ 26 ⊐
27		⊏ 27 ⊐
28		⊏ 28 ⊐
29		⊏ 29 ⊐
30		⊏ 30 ⊐

Turn over for parts 3 - 6 →

SAMPLE

Part 3		Do not write here
31		⊐ 31 ⊏
32		⊐ 32 ⊏
33		⊐ 33 ⊏
34		⊐ 34 ⊏
35		⊐ 35 ⊏
36		⊐ 36 ⊏
37		⊐ 37 ⊏
38		⊐ 38 ⊏
39		⊐ 39 ⊏
40		⊐ 40 ⊏
41		⊐ 41 ⊏
42		⊐ 42 ⊏
43		⊐ 43 ⊏
44		⊐ 44 ⊏
45		⊐ 45 ⊏
46		⊐ 46 ⊏

Part 4		Do not write here
47		⊐ 47 ⊏
48		⊐ 48 ⊏
49		⊐ 49 ⊏
50		⊐ 50 ⊏
51		⊐ 51 ⊏
52		⊐ 52 ⊏
53		⊐ 53 ⊏
54		⊐ 54 ⊏
55		⊐ 55 ⊏
56		⊐ 56 ⊏
57		⊐ 57 ⊏
58		⊐ 58 ⊏
59		⊐ 59 ⊏
60		⊐ 60 ⊏
61		⊐ 61 ⊏

Part 5		Do not write here
62		⊐ 62 ⊏
63		⊐ 63 ⊏
64		⊐ 64 ⊏
65		⊐ 65 ⊏
66		⊐ 66 ⊏
67		⊐ 67 ⊏
68		⊐ 68 ⊏
69		⊐ 69 ⊏
70		⊐ 70 ⊏
71		⊐ 71 ⊏
72		⊐ 72 ⊏
73		⊐ 73 ⊏
74		⊐ 74 ⊏

Part 6									
75	A	B	C	D	E	F	G	H	I
76	A	B	C	D	E	F	G	H	I
77	A	B	C	D	E	F	G	H	I
78	A	B	C	D	E	F	G	H	I
79	A	B	C	D	E	F	G	H	I
80	A	B	C	D	E	F	G	H	I

151

UNIVERSITY *of* CAMBRIDGE
Local Examinations Syndicate

SAMPLE

Candidate Name
If not already printed, write name
in CAPITALS and complete the
Candidate No. grid (in pencil).

Candidate's signature

Examination Title

Centre

Supervisor:
☒ If the candidate is ABSENT or has WITHDRAWN shade here ▭

Centre No.

Candidate No.

**Examination
Details**

0	0	0	0
1	1	1	1
2	2	2	2
3	3	3	3
4	4	4	4
5	5	5	5
6	6	6	6
7	7	7	7
8	8	8	8
9	9	9	9

Listening Comprehension Answer Sheet

Enter the test number here ▭▭▭

For office use only ⊏3⊐ CPE ⊏5⊐ CAE ⊏0⊐⊏1⊐⊏2⊐⊏3⊐⊏4⊐⊏5⊐⊏6⊐⊏7⊐⊏8⊐⊏9⊐
⊏0⊐⊏1⊐⊏2⊐⊏3⊐⊏4⊐⊏5⊐⊏6⊐⊏7⊐⊏8⊐⊏9⊐

Write your answers below	Do not write here	Continue here	Do not write here
1	▭ 1 ▭	21	▭ 21 ▭
2	▭ 2 ▭	22	▭ 22 ▭
3	▭ 3 ▭	23	▭ 23 ▭
4	▭ 4 ▭	24	▭ 24 ▭
5	▭ 5 ▭	25	▭ 25 ▭
6	▭ 6 ▭	26	▭ 26 ▭
7	▭ 7 ▭	27	▭ 27 ▭
8	▭ 8 ▭	28	▭ 28 ▭
9	▭ 9 ▭	29	▭ 29 ▭
10	▭ 10 ▭	30	▭ 30 ▭
11	▭ 11 ▭	31	▭ 31 ▭
12	▭ 12 ▭	32	▭ 32 ▭
13	▭ 13 ▭	33	▭ 33 ▭
14	▭ 14 ▭	34	▭ 34 ▭
15	▭ 15 ▭	35	▭ 35 ▭
16	▭ 16 ▭	36	▭ 36 ▭
17	▭ 17 ▭	37	▭ 37 ▭
18	▭ 18 ▭	38	▭ 38 ▭
19	▭ 19 ▭	39	▭ 39 ▭
20	▭ 20 ▭	40	▭ 40 ▭